THE FIRST FLAG

THE FIRST FLAG

SARAH FOX

 COFFEE HOUSE PRESS • MINNEAPOLIS • 2013

Coffee House Press books are available to the trade through our primary distributor, Consortium Book Sales & Distribution, cbsd.com or (800) 283-3572. For personal orders, catalogs, or other information, write to: info@coffeehousepress.org.

Coffee House Press is a nonprofit literary publishing house. Support from private foundations, corporate giving programs, government programs, and generous individuals helps make the publication of our books possible. We gratefully acknowledge their support in detail in the back of this book.

Good books are brewing at coffeehousepress.org

LIBRARY OF CONGRESS
CATALOGING-IN-PUBLICATION DATA

Fox, Sarah, 1966–
The first flag / Sarah Fox.
p. cm.
ISBN 978-1-56689-326-8 (pbk.)

I. Title.

PS3606.O9565F57 2013

811'.6—DC23

2012036533

PRINTED IN THE UNITED STATES

FIRST EDITION | FIRST PRINTING

For my daughter, Nora Catherine Wynn

PREFACE: DIFFICULTY AT THE BEGINNING

ONE: OBJECT RELATIONS

1   Daughter Object
3   Transitional Object
6   Fata Morgana
8   Before Completion
11 Muse Object
13 Wife Object
15 The Clinging, Fire
18 Holding Together [Union]

TWO: PROJECTIVE IDENTIFICATION

29 Dispersion [Dissolution]
34 My Helmet: A Sonnet
35 The Marrying Maiden
39 My Sword Loves Me
41 The Arousing (Shock, Thunder)
44 My Antler
51 After Completion
55 War on Drugs
57 Biting Through
60 Moms vs. Dads

THREE: COMMA

(1)

69 *I Slid Out of My Mother's Body*
69 *Exogeny*
69 *Eros, Indiscriminate*
70 *Coma*

70   *Doll Box*

70   *Brain Letter*

71   *A Woman Waits for Me*

71   *Merge*

71   *Satellite*

     (II)

72   *Dr. Kronos*

72   *Born in Prison*

73   *Disease*

73   *Quarantine*

73   *I Don't Want*

74   *Side Effects*

74   *Satchidananda*

74   *Dying of Darkness*

     (III)

75   *Bondage*

75   *Transference*

75   *Couch*

76   *Poetry as Magic*

76   *The Other Husband*

76   *Raccoon*

77   *Ambassador*

77   *Little Boy Lost*

77   *Kairos*

     (IV)

78   *Centrifuge*

78   *More Cloudy Places*

78   *Poison Path*

79   *Psyche, Unraveling*

79   *Skull Collector*

79 *Kula*

80 *Sacrifice*

80 *Inside the Deer*

FOUR: THE TOWER

87 Essay on Patriarchy

88 Essay on My Tower

90 Essay on My Tower (2)

92 Essay on My Memory

97 Essay on My Fathers

101 Essay on Time

108 Essay on Increase

FIVE: THE CALDRON

117 Decorum of the House

120 A Kiss is a Kiss Named Little Apple

122 The Animal in Me

126 Naked

142 Placental Economics

144 The Joyous, Lake

146 Postnatural

150 Acknowledgments

In fact, the placenta of the pharaoh was placed on a pole and carried into battle. This is history's first flag.
—LLOYD DEMAUSE, "The Fetal Origins of History"

Though my rule for this poem /
is honesty, my other rule is fuck you.
—ALICE NOTLEY, *Disobedience*

PREFACE

DIFFICULTY AT THE BEGINNING[1]

THE IMAGE

Clouds and Thunder
The image of DIFFICULTY AT THE BEGINNING
Thus the superior person^2
Brings order out of Confusion
—I CHING

Astrology is an ancient art and science . . . based on the doctrine
of universal sympathy. *—STANISLAV GROF*

SABIAN SYMBOLS[3]

15 Virgo (Uranus/Pluto conjunction): In the Zoo, Children are Brought Face to Face with an Orangutan

18 Virgo (Ascendant): An Ouija Board

20 Scorpio (Neptune): A Woman Draws Away Two Dark Curtains Closing the Entrance To a Sacred Pathway

25 Scorpio (South Node): American Indians Making Camp After Moving into a New Territory

15 Sagittarius (Imum Coli): Seagulls Fly Around a Ship in Expectation of a Flood

14 Pisces (Moon): A Lady Wrapped in a Large Stole of Fox Fur

18 Pisces (Descendant): A Master Instructing His Disciple

26 Pisces (Chiron): Watching the Very Thin Moon Crescent Appearing At Sunset, Different People Realize that the Time Has Come to Go Ahead with their Different Projects

28 Pisces (Saturn): Light Breaking Into Many Colors as it Passes Through a Prism

11 Taurus (Venus): A Woman Watering Flowers in Her Garden

25 Taurus (True Node): A Spanish Gallant Serenades His Beloved

9 Gemini (Mars): An Airplane Performing a Nose Dive

12 Gemini (Pars Fortuna): A Famous Pianist Giving a Concert Performance

15 Gemini (Medium Coli): A Woman Activist In An Emotional Speech Dramatizing Her Cause

19 Gemini (Sun): A Large Archaic Volume Reveals a Traditional Wisdom

5 Cancer (Mercury): Game Birds Feathering Their Nests

7 Cancer (Jupiter): A Group of Rabbits Dressed in Human Clothes Walk as if on Parade

DIFFICULTY AT THE BEGINNING

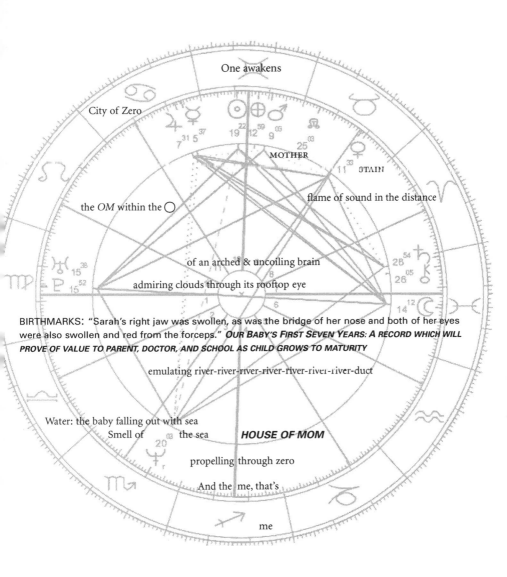

One awakens

City of Zero

MOTHER

OTAIN

the OM within the ○

flame of sound in the distance

of an arched & uncoiling brain

admiring clouds through its rooftop eye

BIRTHMARKS: "Sarah's right jaw was swollen, as was the bridge of her nose and both of her eyes were also swollen and red from the forceps." *OUR BABY'S FIRST SEVEN YEARS: A RECORD WHICH WILL PROVE OF VALUE TO PARENT, DOCTOR, AND SCHOOL AS CHILD GROWS TO MATURITY*

emulating river-river-river-river-river-river-river-duct

Water: the baby falling out with sea
      Smell of   the sea   *HOUSE OF MOM*

propelling through zero

And the me, that's

me

NOTES

[1] DIFFICULTY AT THE BEGINNING: Hexagram 3, *Chun*. *I Ching, or Book of Changes: The Richard Wilhelm Translation (rendered into English by Cary F. Baynes)*. Bollingen Foundation: Princeton University Press: 1950 (16–17).

[2] I substitute the word "person" for Wilhelm's "man."

[3] The "Sabian Symbols" consist of 360 images, corresponding to all 360 degrees of the zodiac, that were channeled in 1925 by the astrologer Marc Edmond Jones with the help of Elise Wheeler, a paraplegic spiritualist medium. The astrologer Dane Rudhyar, in his book *An Astrological Mandala: The Cycle of Transformations and its 360 Day Symbolic Phases,* described the Sabian Symbols as a "contemporary American embodiment of the *I Ching.*" The symbols remain in use among contemporary astrologers; those quoted correspond to my own natal chart.

1.

OBJECT RELATIONS

Here we have the fundamental concept in the Book of Changes.
The 8 trigrams . . . represent a family consisting of a father,
mother, three sons, and three daughters . . .
not objective entities but functions.
—RICHARD WILHELM

❀

The family is society in embryo.
—I CHING

❀

Our psyche is set up in accord with the structure of the universe,
and what happens in the macrocosm likewise happens in the
infinitesimal and most subjective reaches of the psyche.
—CARL JUNG

DAUGHTER OBJECT

*All religions contain at their center the Suffering Fetus and its
Poisonous Placenta.* —Lloyd DeMause

In his efforts to improve her, my father
removed a gland from my mother's
entrails. Helmeted by her hair hive and pretty
penny-eyes, she found his intrusion a thrilling
privilege. He, who soared like a cliff face
before the perceived paucity of her inner
dross and dirt-infested origins. She whose
very organs reeked of streetswill and bogmoss.

To this gland he applied all the instruments
and potions of his trade. He blew through it
a wind from his youth and caressed its thickening
hide. He placed it on a dish in the sunshine and thus
did he grow me. I pleasured him with the cuteness
of my body's primitive neutrality and the soft
pink swoons nimbling from my flowerthroat.
I toddled around in the dish sphere, highlighted.

Meanwhile the sun's measured glance began
to cinder and curl my proliferating mechanics.
I acquired folds and lobes, a misshapen middle
part mottled by holes he had neglected to suture
so that the outside air with its mother dust
entered, deformed, and blighted me. My father

found himself repulsed, and finally indifferent.
He hung me to cure in a tree. The birds

strung me up with mysteries, dark cravings—
wove nests from my hair, sang through me.
I was a bird brothel, atremble; I was too much frenzy
under the moon my father dreaded in passing
and shunned. Father-shadowed entities gaze,
they root and coil and hunger, tongue my every
aspect. If they weren't the only him I had
I'd ask the birds to peck out their eyes.

TRANSITIONAL OBJECT

The glass or vessel is called Mother. —PARACELSUS

I watched myself being dragged across a bleak terrain
inside a cage made of bones. The bones must have
belonged to a very large animal, possibly human,
possibly even my mother. The man dragging me kept
apologizing for locking me up and for dragging me
across this treeless corpse of a landscape. It was as if
he could not stop dragging me around, he simply
could not let me out of the cage made of the bones
of my mother, until I had accepted his apology
for hauling me everywhere inside the cage
made of the bones of my mother. I realized
I was expected to say something—I
wasn't sure what, maybe "it's okay" or
"you were right to put me inside this cage
made of the bones of my mother, I belong
here"—but I also knew that we'd both *know*
that I didn't really believe it, and so I'd only come
off as unreliable, thus even more monstrous,
by saying what he seemed really to want me to say—
in the sense, for example, of "I just adore
being your nurse," or "Thanks a bunch," or "You're
going to go to Heaven, honey." He
kept apologizing and I was aware of myself
struggling to articulate the *general sentiment*
I hoped I had correctly guessed I was expected

to convey, maybe more along the lines of: "I'm sorry
you feel so sorry for putting me in this cage
made of the bones of my mother." And then
it dawned on me that I didn't have a voicebox—
in the area where sound might form I sensed mere air.
I wondered if the cage made of the bones of my mother
correlated to my voicebox, like a flag;
and then I wondered if thought for the voiceless
could amass like a ghost-talk, and if he'd hear me thinking
how pathetic I found his relentless apologizing. I began
to focus on changing my thoughts, if only to project
onto my face how sorry I was that he felt so sorry
for having surgically removed my voicebox,
and for locking me up inside a cage made
of the bones of my mother, and for carting
me across this abysmal plain covered with endless
anthills and crabgrass. And: that I was sorry
for my confounding, inappropriate nakedness,
which unavoidably obliged him to indulge his
urge upon the roof of my mother's sharp bones. I
was sorry that he couldn't help it and sorry that he felt
so sorry for screaming and spitting at my face,
its actual bones still reverberating from his hack job.
For Christ's sake didn't I understand how much he *loved* me,
loved this cage made especially for me out of the bones
of my very own mother? And I thought, "Okay."
I thought this with great concentration, I thought it
so forcefully that I think I actually began to think it.
And he said, "I'm sorry that I have to spend *my life*
yoked to that cage made of Mother's bones—

all I ever wanted was a muse, a natural nanny.
Who'd aspire to drag a hag around in a cage made of her
very own bones?" And I thought, "Oh." And I thought,

"Oh yeah." And I started to change within
our/self. I started to project into the space of my mother
a thought: *my bones*. And I changed my thoughts
about "mother" & "cage" & "meadow," & then
"daughter." And "I am" & "he's not." And I imagined
a *Yes* that birthed out a star pour, each bone recomposing
as skyward colostrum. I thought body & dirt,
bloodstream & bilirubin. I thought ovum,
menstruum, ectoplasm, miasma, utopian tubes.
And I thought larva, chakra, animal, embryo,
placenta, the migrating clouds, the treetops.

FATA MORGANA

We came on this trek to find our life, for we are all the
children of a flaming flower. —RAMÓN MEDINA SILVA

I trek through the desert to find my life.
I am so small and bright, a living kingdom, irrigated
and stockpiled. Feelings and forms needle
through me like plankton riding a river. The river *in me*
is compatible with twenty-first-century platforms,
like the river in you. I swallow with a good swallow,
a tall glass. How did I get to be so small?

I notice that the desert is deader than other dead things.
Loamier corpses retain some syrup, can be bent, will give
when pressed: more like live bodies than dead
desiccated wisps of ash. More like a love shack
where I offer myself like a wet nurse to the furry
feline comma vanishing on the dune. Her death
is my favorite moment of our acquaintance.
I observe death leak curriculum according
to proximity, to volume. Corpse-touching
as medicine. I invite this dearly departing cutie-pie
to cozy me up while I graze her with my cuticles
(as with a blankie). It's true that I went to the desert

to find my mystagogy, as others do: "It is very clear
that Jesus refused to turn the desert stones into bread."[1]
Amma Sarah, forgotten desert mother, proclaimed

of the desert, "I put out my foot to ascend the ladder,
and place death in front of my eyes before going up it."[2]
Jesus refused each temptation. "Not live by bread alone."
The forgotten peyote mothers claim the desert a cosmic
portal. Their temptation—desert flower—"is everything
that is." Their temptation—"is beautiful because it is right."
"There is no one who regrets what we are."[3]

What I keep meaning to say is: I saw the tracings
of my very own death mask pressed into the sand.
It was tempting, it was worth the risk. I knelt down
to scoop it up, but my face fell apart in my hands.

BEFORE COMPLETION[4]

THE JUDGMENT: *[I]f the little fox, after nearly completing the crossing, / Gets his tail in the water, / There is nothing that would further.* —I CHING

We made it to the church alive.
See the rabbits fucking?
I am full of rabbit and have no edge.
But apparently I survive. Breathing,
my earth status rapidly unravels.
An other father
offers to embrace me (this is no
longer a church). Sadly, he's
imaginary. If he traded places
then someone else would be
imaginary instead.
Does visual matter hold steady? Am I

even a thought pattern? This is the mind
on drugs—apocalyptic,
or "Heart of the House"—where
I hit my limit. (Even just one hit hurts.)

He's not going to get a new heart.
(*That's the heart of the matter.*) I scan
my thoughts for his vacant chest,
imagine a severed heart in somebody's
hand. If I could keep

the sight of him steady I would
stick my fist through the hole sawed
into his ribcage and form a pretend
organ. Grind it in there, pumping. I'm in
a space jam. Heart trouble. And then,

the teacher said, "inhale forward
into plank." She said, "fill your heart
space with gratitude."
"This is our national joy."[5]
The imaginary father dangled
a root in my hand.
It felt like holding testicles—each
little tail a perfect whisker.

(Last time I dug up roots I hit
an ants' nest.) Just getting hit one
time is not really such a big deal.
I am only in this fucking hospital
for the endorphins. (I just took one
hit, for old times' sake.)(*I made it
to the hospital alive.*) The solstice moon

pretends to be a cross in the sky.
It's like the third eye of God
the boy, only rabbitish. I'm apparently
in my yard. I transplant some peonies
over the ants' nest. My hands work
better than a trowel to feel for the root
tails, snapping them up like a hem seam.

I don't want to stunt them.
I want to hold the whole
thing in my palm, a live
wet heart pulsing against
my finger like a rabbit.

It's so hard to get to the bottom of it.

MUSE OBJECT

The caterpillar and Alice looked at each other for some time in silence.
—LEWIS CAROLL
>   *Nobody wants to be the muse; / in the end everyone wants to be*
>   *Orpheus.* —LOUISE GLÜCK

we continue this middle,
colliding as wave
                    under boat —
        our speechnotspeech trolls

                    for a child who can begin again,
                    not in bloodboil but as *rockabyebabyboat*
                            as a posy atavistic verbs (who is the you?)

avatars of the fantasy wander
the atmosphere
in search of little creatures   we've plainly sighted

        who tolerate thorny boundaries based on Old World *nos*
(and the poem hanging there in some noose, anchorless)
        (blood rising in the trees, the wind of distances passes me

        your gaze its chime)

                        — bliss of proximity — but —

what's really wrong we know to be commonplace:
                    love edges the room,

room in the boat for an idea of love
w/o punishment & Eros flying . . .

there's a core delight in disclosure, a hunger that follows,
death of the hour,
trees, beautiful, are also dying

you fold up like a gate, limby apparatus, and
bring absence into its paradox

cannot want that moment   pursue you — unwillingly — w/
pieces of ocean in my eyes, mindgaze
maze

the middle triangulates that haunting we recognize

that vertigo

tide abuses the border between one thought
and its failed expression
where space amasses,

translates the acts of a mind at the edge of itself

at the juncture of co-observation —
hiding into our gaze, like that

one moves while the other views / *I worry
that my I is not what I think it is*

I want
a quiet speculation to quarrel
as consolation for your always underwaterness

WIFE OBJECT

By the time my symbols reached the other
you, goldenly, I was elsewhere, "reported threat,"
you know, quietly. I, unsorry & story
wise, wanted a snake. An exact right. *Mine.*
Her increased range over our little hole. This world
is made by clearing what I'm doing, watch past
doors cry open or break, sunlight not paying
any mind. Feeling fine, then I reach into
the cellar of my face. "Wait," I said, "you said I was,
I was her." Canyon . . . You always end up weeping
when I'm not around, always flaunting fake
symbolism knowing words can be like that. Roaming
among used stones, tender mountain spirits, I recognize
which antique principles I'm clearing, which rights.
Themselves are partly made up (by you). (Right?).
When I was a little girl a chunk of rock
was like that, like you: part emotion part dark ("chiasmus").
Fluid damp circles: not so. No exchange
of power through retaining wall. Place I slice open
if you say don't (*TELL*). You, featured as a church
nearly, full of naked submission. I said I
was afraid but I wasn't. My own original
symbol's better now, and cuz I don't want to. I
keep searching the building for our furniture
and for Joan of Arc. I try to mine the goldbits of *mine*
vis-á-vis intersubjective homestead hoax [love]
[nest] [ablaze]. But wife wind, like a detonated wing,
storms off with gold of me coiled so depressed,

I wanted a real alone—layers & layers. Diffuse
pathologies family-treeing all up in my business.
Your couch, your steeple, your Tuesdays at 10.
I future us another somewhere with purest thought.
You said, "I have two wives" to someone, what did
you say? Am I not for saying to ever? Instead she's.

THE CLINGING, FIRE⁶

Fire has no definite form but clings to the burning object and thus is bright. —I CHING

*Fire is thus a privileged phenomenon which can explain anything . . .
It is cookery and it is apocalypse . . . It is a tutelary and a terrible
divinity.* —GASTON BACHELARD, *The Psychoanalysis of Fire*

Buried at the bottom of fire is fire's absence.
You will never find anything else, even
if you wait, or lavish the fire with a primal
kiss, or promise to stow it inside you
while fasting under the full moon; even
if you pray. Or even wax your subtle ego
to a fierce luster, rub and rub and rub.
Later, you fall asleep in a flower while watching
a movie about a fire, and in the light
of day you wonder if you're supposed to feel
embarrassed for witching the dance floor
at your own wedding, for disclosing
to the smokers of cigarettes and opium
that you felt flame shafting out of your fingertips
like torch lighters, like, you said, extensions
of your body at a molecular level,
and you said that you'd discovered how to sweep
dread away with your killer mudras—*Pwah!*
Someone offers a card that reads WARNING:
Do Not Set Self On Fire. But you're high on cosmic

forecasts and the red harmonic promise spanning
the entirety of night. Later still, you wake
up at the bottom of a pond whose skin flickers
with familiar forms that turn out only to be clouds.
There's no fire at the bottom of a pond, nor,
in this one, any fish. Still, you inhabit the atmosphere
like a fish surfacing to suck. Outside, a drunk
stranger collapses and weeps in the yard where once
was fire. He shouts at the sky: *I don't want to live
in God's neighborhood anymore!* Is he crying?
No, you think, he's just peeing his pants.
You go toward the door—to spook him—and trip,
as usual, over the cat, her white glint and wailing.
But then you remember that the cat had perished,
the night before your wedding. You buried
her behind the pond, her stiff little blacked-out
eyes left to linger—just in case—left
to taste the last lick of sun, one last brow beating.
They say we desire containment, and that bodies
do not persist. They say raccoons steal our flesh,
our fish, and our fires. You find a vase of flowers
on the mantle in place of your daughter. You fear
you've been too casual about biology, too
"experimental." You flick your fingers to flint up fire,
but only spit out a feral mist. All sorts of dazzling
objects are replaced by their negatives—reverberating
holes swelling in front of you like space cysts.
Hello, you want to say, *do you speak English?*
You remember a wedding, probably your own.
You had fire in the palm of his hand, in the blink

of your eye. At the bottom of every wedding
is a burial. Even the whimpering vagrant's been reduced
to a scorched silhouette in the grass. Or is that a rosebush?
On the outskirts of every sleep is sleep's shadow,
a residue your fingers slip through reaching for all
the final words that daily no longer exist. Looking for
the lighted parts, the persistent face, the fire's forgiveness
around places on your body you've never seen before.
Who will tell you what to do? *Tell me what to do.*

HOLDING TOGETHER [UNION]⁷

What is required is that we unite with others, in order that all may complement and aid one another through holding together.
—I CHING

It's a lunar eclipse on the Winter Solstice.
Still dark, too cloudy.
We go outside and look up anyway.
It's our tenth anniversary,
we probably should.
Shouldn't everybody?
People are coming over for a party.

Are you a red family or a lunar one?
I should worry about my father.
I'm pretty sure that I worry about my father
but it's hard to tell. My feelings are complicated.
I am *Premenstrual Syndrome* & "*Pseudo-dementia.*"
He is *Rheumatoid Arthritis* & *Congestive Heart Failure,*
T-shaped uterus — *Lumbar stenosis w/ fusion* . . .
The ring John gave me as an anniversary present

is too big, I'm surprised that everything is always so big!
John believes I harbor a distorted image of myself.
I also believe this, like in more ways than one, yet
I continue to hold the image like it's
my baby
that otherwise will dissolve through my fingers

and I just want to hold it
so close to me, offer my nipple to this gazing
infant, *I'll be your mirror, darling.*
                    Bliss latch.
I love you my helpless, papery deception.

Paula brought us a mirror.

        It seems ludicrous to me
        that I am constantly so pathologically late.
        It makes me feel like killing myself.

We were all waiting
for Fred, who was coming from Germany. The paper-bag
lanterns that John & Nora & I painted with esoteric symbols
still glowed when Fred finally arrived. I was asleep.
Mercury's in retrograde and blizzards are happening all over the place!

Eric, who with Kelly arrived precisely on time to our anniversary party,
suggested to me that my drawing of the Hanged Man
from the Tarot indicated that "you're becoming a shaman."
Which, obviously, it does not.
It obviously points to the condition of which chronic lateness is a symptom.

Paula drew the Hierophant, and her husband
Jack drew the Moon (shaman anyone?)
Appropriately, Kelly drew the Magician,
Nora the Fool, and John the Wheel
of Fortune. Eric drew the Empress.
As a couple for our anniversary we drew the Chariot.

THE JUDGMENT

HOLDING TOGETHER brings good fortune:
Inquire of the oracle once again
whether you possess sublimity, constancy, and perseverance.
Then there is no blame.

It's our tenth anniversary, but hardly anyone came to our party.
We tentatively planned to renew our vows and predictably did not.
Instead, we consulted the *I Ching.*

> *Those who are uncertain gradually join.*
> *Whoever comes too late*
> *Meets with misfortune.*

I believe in the path of least resistance, even if that includes misfortune.

> "The Chariot goes where it will and is subject
>   to no power but its own."[8]

> "That cloud looks just like the archetypal / Loss of innocence.
>   I know where you keep the little key to your journal."[9]

> > *The waters on the surface of the earth flow together*
> > *wherever they can.*

Lost souls all over the place as far as anyone knows,
surfing the blood-orbs like constellated gods-eyes.
I wonder if I might be wrong about the market becoming obsolete.

What does money have to do with anniversaries, eclipses,
poetry, lost souls, or any of this?

(As for my epitaph [in case you were wondering,
because I just thought of it
and aren't people supposed to write this stuff down, prepare
a last will & testament filed in some obvious place, such as here?
Because, e.g., "I don't even know if your father
wants to be buried or cremated." If I'm cremated,
can I still have an epitaph? Like, maybe for the program?
Will anyone come to my funeral? Will I have a funeral, if I'm cremated?
Although as of today I'd prefer not to
be cremated, or embalmed, or boxed, and frankly
I'd really prefer not to die.]: *She Wondered Why,* is my epitaph.
Or: *I Wonder Why?*—whichever sounds best.)

Meanwhile, a mnemotic shadow—gleaming onyx orb—slices the sky.
It's moon-mirrored, the beautiful lakes and oceans, like marriage—
an eclipse—sun + moon.
We went out to look at the sky and intuited
a pink essence beyond the clouds.

(This is now the highlight of the poem.)

I may be the only one who perceives the lunar eclipse as placentalesque.
Maybe I'm grasping for straws.
Because lately I've been swaddled in the sorrows of the world,
and I'm always "about to get my period."
Radical anthropologists claim PMS was and is
the catalyst for human revolution. Those are the kind of people.

No country for PMS, or mourning,
or probably most of your shit and everyone's.
No babies, either, for me, for us, for anybody mentioned, for now.

Then the party, the solstice, and the eclipse were over.
We moved on to the other parties.
And I *finally* got my period—a startled
discharge, like lava burping over a caldera,
like the drop of cosmic drama the moon made
passing red through the shadow of the earth—
the very moment I saw the face of my mother

on Christmas Eve, in Waukesha, Wisconsin,
where I belong not, yet persevere.

NOTES

[1] This, along with "not live from bread alone," are adapted from Luke 4: 1–4

[2] *The Sayings of the Desert Fathers (Apophthegmata Patrum: The Alphabetical Collection)*, trans. by Benedicta Ward (Cistercian Publications: 1984).

[3] This and preceding quotes regarding the peyote hunt come from *People of the Peyote: Huichol Indian History, Religion, and Survival*, edited by Stacy B. Schaefer and Peter T. Furst (University of New Mexico Press: 1997).

[4] BEFORE COMPLETION: Hexagram 64, *Wei Chi* (Wilhelm, 248–249)

[5] Elena Brower, June 23, 2010, heard during live streaming of world-record event gathering ten thousand yogis for practice together in Central Park. Elena materialized as a profoundly significant teacher in my daughter Nora's life—after she and I took Elena's class at Virayoga Studio in SoHo, NYC—the very day I sat with Marina Abramovic (5/21/10).

[6] THE CLINGING, FIRE: Hexagram 30, *Li* (Wilhelm, 118–119)

[7] HOLDING TOGETHER (UNION): Hexagram 8, *Pi* (Wilhelm, 36–37)

[8] Dr. Robert Wang, *Jungian Tarot* (Marcus Aurelius Press: 2001).

[9] Nick Demske, *Nick Demske* (Fence Books: 2010).

2.

PROJECTIVE
IDENTIFICATION

Projective identification is a phantasy of projecting the whole,
or a part of, oneself into another object,
taking possession of it, and attributing to the object
one's own characteristics.
—Hanna Segal, *Biography of Melanie Klein*

Projective identification . . . would appear to be
a feature of the economy of all fanatics.
—Marjorie Brierly,
"Further Notes on the Implications of Psycho-analysis"

Somebody just asked me . . . how I felt about Washington.
What a good question, what a good question. Um,
Washington's groovy, ha-ha—and it is—if you're Roman!
—Richie Havens, "All Along the Watchtower,"
live at the Cellar Door, Washington, DC

It's necessary to maintain a state of
disobedience against . . . everything.
—Alice Notley

DISPERSION [DISSOLUTION][1]

*Egotism and cupidity isolate men. Therefore the hearts of men must
be seized by devout emotion.* —RICHARD WILHELM

Resolving to dream of peaceable kingdoms,
I hear "pieceable." I consider that Martin Buber's
"I and Thou" is not really the same as Whitman's "I & You."
Eileen Myles's "Eliot Weinberger can suck my ass," likewise,
may not correspond to Eliot Weinberger's "Alas Eileen."[2]
Though in my dream, Eileen Myles hands me a voodoo
charm with *EM* on one side and *EW* on the other.
It's Relational Magma, or Magnetism.

But I mean really what is it with poets?
Because litmus nucleus failure, how bright
the tongue glows for love.
"The Creative is round, it is the prince, the father,
jade, metal, cold, ice; it is deep red, a good horse,
an old horse, a lean horse, a wild horse, tree fruit."[3]

I sought my harness in a tree
but was assigned, instead, a man.
I wasn't asked.

MB: "Each man must find his central wish."[4]
Is each woman, like each animal,
a *not*-Thou & *not*-I?

"Not-I and Sock-eye went out in a boat.
Sock-eye fell out, who was left?"

I am a swimmer.
I am an animal.
I'm red and waxy and yes I do
wish for

peaceable kings, dispersing.

But also I want a little more,
like all animals—
don't you want anything?
I'm still looking for my central wish: its tenor & vehicle,
my own private Everyday Eleusis.

>   "The mother functions as a default setting
>   for the formulating of the I-you
>   relationship in general,"[5] wrote
>   Barbara Johnson (about Sylvia & Aurelia
>   Plath). Martin Buber died exactly sixteen months
>   after Sylvia Plath, he was 87.
>   He did not melt his brain in an oven
>   like some kind of potatohead. "Unspecified"
>   is all Google can deliver as to the cause of Martin Buber's
>   death, along with "Joy impressed him."
>   I've neglected to read
>   Martin Buber, for no good reason,
>   but am ceaselessly reading Sylvia Plath. "One
>   of the great thinkers of this century," claimed

the NYT— Oh, I'm talking about Buber,
not Plath. I don't recall ever having seen
the term "great thinker" applied to Sylvia
Plath. More quite the opposite, at least
in terms of her own death—"Whack-
job!" *Ach, du Daddy* is not really the same
as *Ich-du God,* but, wrote MB: "Everyone
must come out of his Exile in his own way."

I am dispensing.
Giving myself under.
Itching myself in a particular order.
Just exactly the same as *You.*
Just exactly the same as it feels like "*You*"
is still a problem,
a bit unadjourned
from the whole ugly burden
of swimming under war-sounding
clouds (but a hundred times louder).

Nobody dreamed me. I recognized
only strangers. And that was when your tears were
sorta thrilling. Because GOD YES YES YES YES.
We aren't going to drown in this New Year.
No animals will be annihilated in the manufacturing of this dream.
Nobody's sticking any heads in any ovens
in the brave new millennium.

I'm not yet behind myself,
I can't get no resolution.

The clouds press me under
and the water's freezing.
Everything's cold & chapped, my skin is frost.
Every night is arctic ugly and hemmed.
Every dream is eyeless.

I'd rather go deaf (than blind).
I remember when it wasn't winter,
and I never got to sleep with anyone.
No angel broke in anyone's kisser.
No brain smoke set off the alarms.

Hi, are you still there?

"The Receptive is the earth, the mother.
It is cloth, a kettle, frugal, it is level,
it is a cow with a calf, a large wagon,
form, the plurality, a shaft . . .
The shaft is the body of a tree."[6]

I unearth a bracket of memory.
Ashes ashes.
There are now angels everywhere.

"The Gentle is wood, wind, the eldest
daughter, the guideline,
work; it is the white, the long, the high;
it is advance & retreat,
the undecided odor."[7]

Substance comes from the mother.
Sometimes obliquely.
I hardly knew anyone.
I hadn't achieved my own way of exiling from Thou.
I forgot to archive those flecks of Heaven.

"*A thousand Mississippi*"

MY HELMET: A SONNET
—for Nick Demske (title by Lucas de Lima)

- Temperature: roughly 88° ("feels like 91") with 51% humidity
- Active Advisory: Flood Alert, "chance of T-storms"
- Date: June 3, 2011
- Current Time: 5:07 PM CST
- Location: 45.006632° lattitude, -93.260292° longitude

Dudeface, my mom's not dead. And I'm not sorry
because I don't want a dead mom. Mine—
I'm not finished needing her. As for my father,
"he is kept alive only by virtue of the myriad

instruments of modern medicine installed in or ingested
by his body," my sister (in a sense) said. I want more attention.
I want a new drug. I wanna hold your hand, homie.
You said, "Hey Bo Peep, don't cancel that gig or it will break my heart."

My dad's ♥ hallucinated my cancellation circa 1979.
Hallucination's not much use here now, even if it's God-ish.
I don't like God, I wish I never heard of him! I am into Dad
Demske and his grand electric skull. "One thing you need to know

about your mother," my mother said, "is: red patent leather shoes."
Bo Peep, WI, where the deer & the dead babies play.

THE MARRYING MAIDEN[8]

Affection as the essential principle of relatedness is of the greatest importance in all relationships in the world. —RICHARD WILHELM

After he entered her breathing, she thought
about the number of openings in her body and about
stomas such as those fashioned by otolaryngologic
surgeons upon victims of corporate tobacco.
"Big Tobacco" I think they say, like an Indian name—
"Tail-between-his-Legs," or "Hole-in-the-Sky."

Smokers with stomas can, if they choose, continue
to smoke cigarettes and, one would assume,
anything else, by sucking smoke through the hole
in their throats. They don't breathe
or even talk through their mouths anymore,
though still eat food the regular way.
They still shape words with their lips, but
the connection between their trachea and mouth is gone,
their voice box is removed by laryngectomy,
and they talk by plugging the stoma hole with their finger
to capture breath and force speech out in a manner
we tried as kids when doing "the low voice."

I don't recall there being a name for that voice,
do you? I suspect we had similar childhoods,
except for me being a girl™. Did you ever do that thing
on long family™ road trips where you plug

and unplug your ears real fast with the window open?
Like hearing the ocean in a seashell. A heartbeat.
Like when boys™ pretend-fist-fight. *Pwah!*
What is that sound? Does it come out of a hole?

I wrote a poem™ called "The Spirit of Music"©
during a family road trip from Wisconsin™
to Virginia™. Our dog had diarrhea in the car
at a Howard Johnson's™ while we were inside
eating hot dogs. At what age does "hot dog" become
embarrassing to say? Probably fourth grade.
I was probably in seventh grade during this road trip,
playing Rush™, maybe, or Stevie Wonder™ on my Walkman™.
I had never heard of Friedrich Nietzsche™
or Wagner™ or anything intellectual and thought, then,
that no one would ever *ever* want to kiss me much less rape me.
For my eighth-grade graduation I wore a white gunnysack™
dress with pearly buttons. It mimicked my First Communion

gown, when I first received the body and blood of Christ™.
The first time I felt raped I was a junior in high school,
I was drinking "wop" at a parents-out-of-town party™.
I always remember the edge of the driveway and square-shaped
shrubs. What I mean is: the boy kept trying
to shove his penis into my mouth—I'm not sure how
I ended up kneeling. I remember windowboxes
full of red geraniums and a basketball hoop
on the garage beneath a big spotlight. A brown house,
maybe the girl who lived there was named Linda?

Surgeons, like my father™, cut holes into peoples' bodies
in order to remove disease, organs, breasts,
babies, appendages, prefrontal cortex connections,
herniated discs, and other objects (it's really nothing
like Operation™—which you must have gotten for Christmas™
one year, like me. Or did you get the Cowboy Ranch™
that year? I can't remember— Surgery is violent
and breathtaking: I've seen the masked man peer
into the belly of a woman and wrest out her baby.
Allegedly many survivors of alien abduction
were born by c-section™—go figure).⁹ Surgeons

also insert things, such as pacemakers™, organs,
metal rods, embryos™, implants, bone grafts,
etc™. Various surgeons insist that the wayward disc
in my cervical spine™ must be surgically removed,
which would entail an incision through my throat.
Some might say the disc corresponds to the fifth chakra™,
which governs talking. Pillow-talking. "That's my penis talking."
Some surgeons could be psychopaths™ who fantasize
about making holes to fuck in unconscious peoples' throats.
No one's going to fuck me in the throat. *Pwah!*

The Urban Dictionary™ has an entry for "stoma toma,"¹⁰
defined by <mikey@mike.fat.world> as "the hole in a person's throat
from smoking too much so its ramming ur penis inside
their hole in their throat to jizz in it—
i stoma tomaed sally last night and it felt good."©

K_____, now a multimillionaire semi–top
exec at a "full-service global investment

banking and securities firm," once rammed
and rammed his cock into my mouth while
I counted all my body's holes—like counting sheep.
Then, I was no longer Sips-Like-a-Deer-Girl
who wouldn't go all the way, who never
turned into a surgeon or millionaire.

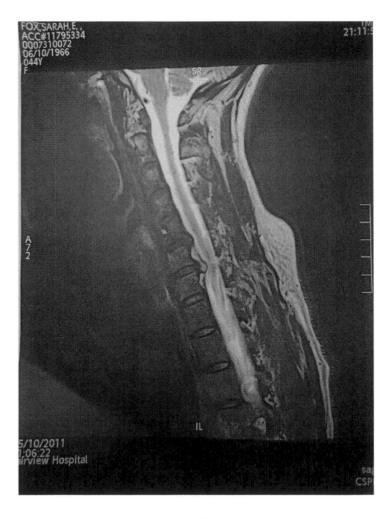

MY SWORD LOVES ME

Every once in a while, I give myself permission
not to feel. I'm always the one who's sobbing
and doing drugs. Emotion, addiction, *why me?*[11]

Why glaciers and matter and the urge to piss?
Why blood, and why not blood? Why sleep, why
rocks by the sea and having to kill, and why does

the little lizard come up to me? I love you,
my ditch flower; I will go with you right now
old man. I'll be apprehendable any day.

I'll grit and bear it truly, I'll be fine. Love
to bleed when you bite into my beauty
tracks, my shame marks; my entire hometown

sang, "No, it didn't hurt. It didn't ovary
a beautiful boy, a beautiful girl, it didn't
switch into a hungry country." *Cut.*

You would be dead now that I've got the sea
out of my eyes. Yes I love to feel your karma touching
my gravestone, I'm as high as a kite.

But this your dream upon our nostalgia
for dead countries and other feelings
partially lit behind smoked glass

representing the heart (of the heart)
attack's circa Bette Davis eyes. Cream
for I SCREAM MY BEAUTIFUL COUNTRY

ENTIRELY, "NO IT DOESN'T HURT"
is what I said. "I don't know how
it happened. I always used to be so young!"

THE AROUSING (SHOCK, THUNDER)[12]

THE JUDGMENT: shock brings success. —I CHING

Then it takes the rest of eternity / to figure out just what the problem was.
—KEVIN CAROLLO

Phew! I thought I was the only one taking eternity
to eat my words, that I alone felt unloved
by the Christcakes and animals I devour the livelong day.
Cannibalism is supposedly the new post-structuralism
and when Rome fell I was twelve years old and still sucked
my thumb. I AM GOING TO WRITE THE REST OF THE POEM
IN ALL CAPS. BECAUSE WHY NOT? I'VE BEEN TO ROME,
I'VE BEEN RAPED, I WASN'T BORN YESTERDAY.
BUT I WILL BE BORN TOMORROW, AGAIN,
TO GREET ANOTHER ROSY DAWN AND TO PAY THE PIPER
FOR PROVIDING THE VIEW. MEANWHILE, 48 GIRLS,
WOMEN, AND BABIES ARE RAPED PER HOUR (RPH)[13]
IN THE DEMOCRATIC REPUBLIC OF CONGO, AND THE VERY MAN
WHO RESCUED HER FROM THE RUBBLE RAPED
A TWELVE-YEAR-OLD HAITIAN GIRL[14] IN THE TENT THEY SHARE
WITH OTHER GIRLS, RAPISTS, AND REFUGEES AMID
THE HEAVILY TOURISTED TENT TOWNS
WHERE HAITIANS STILL NEGOTIATE A SURVIVAL
ECONOMICS[15] DESPITE THE $100 I TEXTED
TO "YELE" @ 501501 THAT'S PROBABLY HELPING COVER
THE COST OF KEEPING WESTERN AID WORKERS COMFORTABLY
AIR-CONDITIONED SO THEY CAN HAVE SEX WHENEVER THEY WANT

IN THE PRIVACY OF THEIR OWN HAITIAN HOLIDAY
INNS. BUT WAIT A MINUTE IS SEX ILLEGAL? IS IT
"AGAINST THE LAW," AS THEY SAY, TO SEXT A PHOTO
OF YOUR WAXY CHEST TO FEMALE FACE-
BOOK "FRIENDS" OR IS IT JUST THAT IT MAKES BILL CLINTON,
WHO OFFICIATED YOUR WEDDING, "DEEPLY UNHAPPY,"
SINCE HE HAS SEXUAL STANDARDS AND FROWNS UPON
"SALACIOUS" OR "EMBARRASSING" SOCIAL NETWORKING FAUX PAS?
IS IT ILLEGAL TO HAVE A BODY, TO FLAUNT YOUR
RAPED & CROOKED, RAW & COOKED BOOTY ON THE STREETS
OF ROME, TO BARE YOUR BONE TO BENEDICT
WHO WILL NEVER NOTICE NO MATTER HOW HARD
YOU TRY TO SODOMIZE SHEEP AND CHILDREN?
EVERYTHING I DO IS PROBABLY ILLEGAL.
EVE ENSLER'S "AHEM MONOLOGUES," SO-CALLED BY CNN
WHEN THEY BANNED USE OF THE WORD
"VAGINA," WAS PANNED BY THE AMERICAN SOCIETY
FOR THE DEFENSE OF TRADITION, FAMILY AND PROPERTY
(TFP) FOR BEING "REPLETE WITH SEXUAL ENCOUNTERS,
LUST, GRAPHIC DESCRIPTIONS OF MASTURBATION,
AND LESBIANISM." THE FACT THAT DSK[16]—
SO-CALLED BY EE—"RAPED AND ATTACKED A HOUSE-
KEEPER IN THE SOFITEL HOTEL[17] IS NOT A SURPRISE,
BASED ON THE HISTORY OF DSK AND THE HISTORY OF MEN
IN POWER AND THE FACT THAT THE MAN HIMSELF
IS THE HEAD OF THE IMF[18], WHICH IS BUSY RAPING AFRICA
ANYWAY. I THINK, YOU KNOW, WOMEN ARE NOT LIKE
SHOCKED BY THAT IDEA."[19] WE'RE NOT LIKE SURPRISED
BY THE IDEA THAT WE'RE PROBABLY GOING TO GET RAPED,
THAT ROME ETERNALLY FALLS ON AND IN OUR BODIES,
IN THE NAME OF THE FATHER, IN THE NAME OF A *HOLY*

GHOST. WE'RE THE RAPEMINES, THE JACKPOT. WE'RE
ARRESTED FOR FEEDING THE HOMELESS IN FLORIDA,
FOR HAVING A MISCARRIAGE IN SOUTH DAKOTA, FOR FAILING
TO LEAVE OUR ABUSIVE BOYFRIEND IN CHICAGO, FOR,
IN A SENSE, GETTING RAPED (AND IF YOU WANT TO
TAKE A MICROSCOPE TO RAPE, LET'S FACE IT
WE'RE ALL TOTALLY FUCKED) IN WISCONSIN.
ARRESTED FOR DANCING AT THE JEFFERSON MEMORIAL—
A NEOCLASSICAL MONUMENT VENERATING ONE OF ROME'S
FOUNDING FATHERS WHO, YOU'LL NOT BE SHOCKED TO HEAR,
FOUND HIS CHARMING SLAVEGIRLS MAGICALLY DELICIOUS.
BUT NOBODY'S PERFECT. THE WAR-TO-ETERNITY BLOWS
LIKE BELUGA THROUGH MANHOLES ON THE BODY OF MOM,
AN EMBRYONIC REFUGEE CAMP WHERE DISASTER
CAPITALISM'S RUNOFF SHRAPNEL TRICKLES DOWN
INTO RESULTANTLY CROOKED OLD VIRGINNIES, WHICH ARE STILL
EVIDENTLY BEGUILING HOLES IN THE WALL TO BE CARRIED BACK TO,
IN THE NAME OF THE FATHER, IN THE NAME OF THE REPUBLIC.
AFTER ALL FOLKS, RAPE IS JUST A 4 LETTER WORD.
SO WHY BOTHER BITCHING ABOUT RAPE OR THE WAR OR WOMBS
FULL OF PLASTIC ARMY GUYS? WHY THE PANIC OVER BEING SLOW,
LATE, UNPATRIOTIC, NAKED, BROKEN-DOWN, HOG-TIED, FORECLOSED, LAID
OFF, SCARED STRAIGHT, THUMBSUCKING & LEFT FOR DEAD ON THE STEPS
OF THE PANTHEON BY METAPHYSICAL POLITICOS BUSY RAPING
ROMAN SHE-WOLVES AND ARCHAIC TORSOS OF APHRODITE?
BECAUSE DEAD IS JUST A 4 LETTER WORD—SO THANK YOU FOR THE WORLD
SO SWEET. THANK YOU FOR THE FOOD WE EAT. IF I SHOULD DIE
BEFORE I WAKE, IT'S OKAY, B/C IT'S MY BIRTH DAY AGAIN TOMORROW.
O I'VE BEEN BORN SO MANY TIMES, O MANY BIRDS WILL SING.

MY ANTLER

The poet Antler wrote me a letter about my book and some recent poems, which I sent him at his request after meeting him at the Celebration of Midwestern Poetry. Antler is a poet from Milwaukee. I am also from Milwaukee, but I never saw Antler when I lived there, and sometimes confused him with Sparrow, who probably has nothing to do with Milwaukee.

I moved to Minneapolis on my twenty-ninth birthday (Saturn Return[20]).

Almost the first thing Antler said to me when I met him was that he had lived with his mother during the month leading up to her death and had, at the end, "birthed her into the next world as she had birthed me into this one." Actually, he didn't say that. He told the story and I suggested the metaphor, probably as some kind of segue into talking about my father or my work as a doula.

Kelly told me she got a contact high just from being next to Antler. I don't know if Antler was actually high. J, Ron Smith, and I went out to the car to smoke hash before the reading component of the Celebration of Midwestern Poetry, after having met Antler. Maybe Kelly meant something different by "high." When I met Antler I could tell that he was mystical, which relaxed me. Antler seemed both trickstery and Gary Snyderesque. While I "knew of him" when I lived in Milwaukee he was, at that time, "crashing on Allen Ginsberg's floor in San Francisco."

Antler appears to be very healthy and glowing, and probably only gets high for ritual or medicinal purposes. I wish I were like that. I wish I were more like Antler.

At the Celebration of Midwestern Poetry, Antler—a featured reader—read a poem about "birthing the mother as she had birthed the son." He abandoned the podium, almost dancing, nearly rollicking: he was all third chakra and "cocks" and Vietnam and "Whitmansexual"—Whitman was *grass-sexual, sleepersexual, corpsewatchsexual, luckier-than-was-thoughtsexual, cosmos-sexual.*[21]

He deserved a standing ovation, which I felt moved solely to give him, but it was one of those readings where the clapping etiquette had not worked itself out. And, being high, I wasn't up to causing a scene. I did, though, feel specially equipped to privately beam my veneration into Antler's brain.

The day after the Celebration of Midwestern Poetry, I sent Antler an e-mail (antlerpoet.net) and told him that I loved him. He e-mailed me back and we shared deer stories, and he said that no, he had never heard of Marina Abramovic. A week after the Celebration of Midwestern Poetry (where I and five fellow panelists—who had been asked to address "The Future of Midwestern Poetry" during a public dialogue with Rob Casper of the Poetry Society of America—more or less evaded the topic), I flew to New York and waited in line at MoMA for two days to sit with Marina Abramović (I made Marina Abramović cry).[22]

It doesn't bother me that Marina Abramović has breast implants. While I would "*never* get breast implants," I confess that I've fantasized about what it might be like. Most of the time, my breasts don't preoccupy me, nor do I pine for their youthful fortitude or any of the other stuff about youth. But I secretly appreciated it when the nurse at the Hope Chest Breast Center referred to me as a "young woman," for whom tumors such as the one noted, on mammogram and ultrasound, at 12:00 in the upper quadrant of my right breast ("1.7 cm hypoechoic mobile mass"), were, in the cases of "young women such as yourself," almost always benign. Sometimes they call it a lesion, and sometimes they even call it a tumor—which doesn't sound benign but apparently, in medical parlance, it occasionally is.

The radiologist, who retrieved five core tissue samples through an intravenous tube puncturing my "mass," told me his brother was a dermatologist. His father had been an obstetrician and his mother a nurse-midwife, which allowed me to segue into my own family's medical lineage, as well as my work as a doula. And when he said I was not to lift anything "bigger than a dinner plate" for twenty-four hours, I told him that if my client went into labor that night—since she was already overdue—I'd have no choice. And then he confused "doula" for, I think, a kind of antidoctor homebirth anarchist, because he said, "Well that's true, I guess if you have to go out and deliver a baby, a baby's bigger than a dinner plate."

People often become mystified by the word "doula." Once when I tried to cross the border into Canada to hike in the virgin pines, a Manitoba border patrolman[23] detained me for four hours and had me strip-searched after I told him I was a doula, and worse, he noted, a doula with tattoos. He scrutinized my bumper stickers, and asked, "Have you ever smoked marijuana in your life?"

Which was confusing, because he was kind of nice at first, and I mean, doesn't Canada even have medical marijuana, and allow the sale of cannabis seeds? I probably said, "Yes, in my lifetime I have smoked marijuana," and that for sure was a mistake. He detained me on the basis of "suspicious plant material" found on the floor of my ("Is this North Korean–made?") car; he scanned every item in my purse with his infrared drug-detecting device. He was really an asshole, he SHOUTED—after finding two Klonopins in a TIC TAC container for which no, I do not have the prescription handy but I'd be happy to call Walgreens, whose number I know by heart, so he could speak with a pharmacist—"WILL THE PHARMACIST AT WALGREENS BE ABLE TO IDENTIFY YOU DOWN TO YOUR TATTOOS? WE DO NOT LET JUST ANYONE WANDER INTO THE SOVEREIGN NATION OF CANADA. PLEASE READ ALOUD THE STATEMENT ON THIS PLAQUE REGARDING YOUR DETAINMENT."

I'm totally serious! And you think those captive Palestinian schoolgirls are a pack of conniving terrorists, and that extraordinary rendition is a fantasy of the "radical left"; you probably also have a "savings account"—sucker. Obviously, he detained me because he hates women, let's not beat around the bush, especially women who call themselves doulas. I only wanted to go for a hike in the virgin pines.

47

I'm like, "Sir, I'm here to teach poetry at the Roseau High School," which, as I'm sure you can guess, ONLY MADE MATTERS WORSE. Roseau is boggy and treeless. I really missed trees. I wanted to walk around in the pines. FUCK THE PATROLMAN AT THE BORDER, every border within and without. *I'M TALKING TO YOU,* he kept saying, but *No one else was around.*

I wonder if "doula" sounds too much like "vagina" combined with something akin to "voodoo," and almost evokes a "feminine sex drool." Much of the time people don't know what a doula is, and seem not to want to know anything about any witchy feminist initiation ceremony type of thing. A thing maybe involving weird placental rites, and women who don't shave their armpits or bathe. When I was his doula, Steve Burt told me that doula is "a Greek word meaning 'female slave,'" and he knows what he's talking about. Microsoft Word, for example, does not recognize "doula" as a word in English usage.

I do shave my armpits, and am on the whole rather vain about my looks. To cut to the chase, last week at a wedding I pulled out my pipe in the parking lot and asked an older sibling of the bride if he minded. He said, "only if you share." (I always share.) After a while he admitted that he'd nailed me as a stoner during the ceremony, which had improved his outlook for the rest of the night. I've been told this before, and it always surprises me. Do I really look like a stoner? How come? Isn't the whole cannabis situation utterly insane? Is my *I* not what I think it is?

The people in line with me at Marina Abramović didn't seem to view me as a stoner, maybe it's not like that in New York. I told someone in line I thought Marina Abramović was "a shaman," which others in our proximity overheard and in the convening line-talk I was designated "the poet" who had "more of a mystical take on what's going on here." In his letter, Antler noted, "it would be hard for adult person to curl up inside gutted deer, but in the dream anything can happen and make sense. Baudelaire miniaturized himself to Tinkerbell size and imagined taking his beloved to see a hideously rotting maggots corpse, he told her 'someday you'll be like that' in hopes it would turn her on to be with him. Hmmm."

Antler writes a lot of addenda sideways along the margins such as: "P.S. I sent some of my gay poems to Raymond Luczak & he sent me *Mute* with a simpatico letter of friendship & solidarity." Also, "*Comma* seems a Paleolithic hallucinogenic dreamstate phantasmagoric shaman voyage," and is "Intense & Real . . . Tell John I'll try to listen to his CD soon and give him some feedback."

The Hope Chest Breast Center nurse wouldn't let John into the biopsy room because "there isn't enough space." I suddenly envisioned the tumor in my breast as analogous to an airbag that, when surgically punctured, might burst out of my body and pin everyone against the mauve wall, and I pictured John's distressing excitement at being smashed by my giant, infested, toxic breast with tubes spraying pus and other gross fluids all over his hair and the machines and the sweet bald doctor whose brother is a dermatologist. Literature in the

"After Care Guide for Breast Biopsy" folder warned: "You may notice bruising in the area of the needle biopsy or sometimes in the lower portion of the breast, the blood will flow with gravity settling at the bottom. This should resolve." I had to wear one of those white gowns that open in front and that had come directly out of a warming device, like an incubator. They really pamper you at the Hope Chest Breast Center.

I like how "hope chest" rhymes with "dope fest." After the radiologist had snapped up five pieces of tissue, and reassured me that "in all likelihood this is going to turn out to be a perfectly benign fibroadenoma," the ultrasound tech showed me the tumor on the screen. "It's that black hole above all the white stuff," she said. I could see there was definitely something there, and that it was filled with a dark archive.

AFTER COMPLETION[24]

When heat is too great, water evaporates into the air.
These elements brought into relation and thus generating
energy are by nature hostile to each other. —RICHARD WILHELM

According to the Kogi Mamas[25], certain beings have cast a shadow
over the Earth. Certain xenophobes in fact eat and piss
in McDonald's all over the world, even in Rome.
I'm not a xenophobe. Last year I ended

my analysis. Bernadette Mayer's psychiatrist
was also named David except she got to ride in her David's
Mercedes *and* kiss him *and* "come
close to making love."[26] In the lingua franca
of the hermetic hour, as it were, that's a serious
score. My David drives either (depending on weather)
an electric moped or the same model "deep navy blue" Ford
Contour John drives, which is like: why the double blue death drive?

David had a dream in which he saw elaborated
Hindu tattoos morphing and speaking on my back.
"We were in our underwear," he said, "and I think
I was just about to give you a back rub."
That intriguing dream nevertheless was the beginning
of the eventual end, last year, of my analysis with David.
It really was the end, the very last one, I had dog shit
on my clog. I, fearless & righteous, *ate him alive.*

(Is that a saying?) Do people still use the word "personality"?
I left a dab of dog shit on his couch. BOUNDARY VIOLATION!

The Kogi Mamas are Harmony Guardians of the Earth.
Some of them favor unleashing the hecatomb, "given the gloomy
disaster of this terrifying situation." Right, which we know.
Harmony might have something to do with Lyric. *Poet*
might have something to do with *Cro-Magnon*.
The Venus of Hohle Fels ("Prehistoric Porn")[27] is
considered the oldest example of figurative art created by humans,
a nearly 40,000-year-old postpartum goddess, a *mother substance*.
And of course she was found in a cave (*hohle fels* = "hollow cave").

The Kogi Mamas (are men) have a euphemism for Dick Cheney,
Marcus Aurelius, Ronald McDonald, and all you all,
which is: "certain beings who have cast a shadow over the Earth."
When David gets nervous a certain shadow passes over
his eyes. He was Mom, King, headless horseman, infant son, the works.
Once in an email he wrote, "As your current father perhaps
it's my job to sign you up for a dance class." Once he wrote,
"Okay, so now for the uncharted waters: As your husband,
it is more clear to me that I am supposed to have needs of you.
I had this same thought with regards to being in the role
of your father, but it's much clearer as a husband."

To make a long story short, I couldn't sustain our separation.
It was *so* the end, I swear, such a graveyard. Lists and consultants.
Anne Carson's Glass Essay. Schopenhauer's Porcupines.
Salvia sessions and the "Other Wife." He wrote,
"I didn't sleep last night. I feel like a piece of shit.

I've been sobbing . . . but I have no intention
of abandoning you." The truth is I've been back
in analysis with David twice a week since summer.
Early in our *relationship*, he wrote, "It sounds to me
like you have been wrestling with a rather fierce dragon
these past few days. I'd like it if you'd bring it into our next
meeting and share the fire and carnage with me.
It's fine if I get burnt or slashed in the process."
David is not a poet but gave his son a Sanskrit name
that means "poet." He said, "You and he are my favorite
poets, no one else can compare." But what does he know?

Foxes are archetypal animals and/or tropes ("cunning like a fox").
I am more cunning than anyone ever thought. But I'm not mean,
or a xenophobe. I legitimately love babies, and I also love you. I do
have a bothersome Electra complex (in case you haven't noticed)—I can't
relate to those girls who cuddle and stroll about with their daddies
and enjoy going to lunch or dancing with them, and so on. But archetypes,
and other psychoanalytic constructs, are no substitute for love.
Nor, it goes without saying, is cunning. I know I'm nobody's
favorite poet, and I was right about David—but it doesn't matter.

In *The Greatest Living Poet*[28], Mark S. Kobo writes, "Young
Faustus / you who winter in the spider's web, who farm /
as undiminished ore of souls." Spiders are also archetypal creatures,
they web & write, and winter-over Young Faustus as a fat dead fly.
I'm not the one who always needs to be right let's just say.
Projective identification, penance, the Object, or whatever.
I know, right? What a weird social contract! The only time
I ever touched David was the day we met, and shook hands.

Surrogate longing, finally, is indescribable. No *there* there.
I'm compliant and polite. I never have bad drunks anymore
and to be honest, David encouraged me to chill out about rules.
I strive, *really* I do. The moon, in the end, seems to have nothing
to do with it. And we all know the moon's not made of cheese
and is not going to do us any good when we're starving
and have run out of babies. "Hecatomb" is a *freaky concept!*
"It is no longer a question of a false representation of reality
but of concealing the fact that the real is no longer real,
and thus of saving the reality principle."[29] Jean Baudrillard
said this on his way to the Pantheon—(and only last night
I finally got it about the Pantheon, its central open eye
in the dome aiming straight at the sun, I finally got why I always loved
that rock-hard temple). I was there when Baudrillard said that.
Or was that you who said it? Which you? Which one of you was it?

WAR ON DRUGS

*Deep in the darkest part of the Forest, the Heroine undergoes Initiation
into the mysteries and magick of the Special World. We can apply this
journey to the cycle of Venus, which corresponds to the 7 gates of
alchemy, and to the myth of Inanna.*
—GARY CATON, The Goddess Astrologer[30]

I was smoking dried ants and toaster crumbs
Could there be anything I wouldn't smoke?
I was freebasing a stash of friendly animals. Then,
Venus returned from the Great Below and shimmered.
My lungs sparkle for Venus, stretch to meet her
way of time. Venus work increases slowly, please remove
your shoes and your clocks. Please shut
up about the fucking taxes, or economy,
or voting, or whatever. What could be worse
than the way it is now? Or better? I smoke
these questions in my mind. Some animals
didn't burn all the way because of the plastic.
They must have been feeding on the lawns.
The friendlier animals nibbled cute mushrooms.
We might all be such friendly consumers.
We might all consummate our covenant with actual
gods. Who cares if I'm smoking a rose thorn
or a beetle wing? Maybe it's the cat's nail tip, or a crow claw.
Crows eat anything and are oily-black like cockroaches.
"We've got a crow family nested in the pine,
which means a baby crow this summer,"

John said. The crows harass me, I'm like, *"yes yes yes*
I know you're here!" But then I notice they're
bitching at another crow, he's trying
to steal their egg. "They do that," John said.
The crows screech and flail and riot, but
they don't stockpile weaponry or torture their foes.
Some foreign crow comes sniffing out their egg:
they flap and shriek, I don't see how they could kill him.
Crows eat crow eggs I guess, but crows don't really eat
actual crows. Do crows eat crows? Do crows kill?
Does anyone actually eat actual crow?
"*Eating crow* is of a family of idioms having to do
with eating and being proved incorrect."
Owls, when provoked, take the heads off crows.
"Crows hate owls." "Crow Season"
is about humans killing varmints. But still,
there are still so many black crows everywhere
in the trees of my neighborhood and in the sky
when I'm driving around and wherever I go. Crows
make me think of Orpheus. Crows make me think
of the Matriarchy. Crows make me want to screech
and flail and smoke. Crows are huge, maybe as big
as hawks. They tend not to die, but maybe they do kill.
According to frequentlyaskedquestionsaboutcrows.com,
"yes crows do kill they are just selfish animal cannibals."
Well, look who's talking! And there are just
still so many shiny black crows all over the world,
and in our yard, and this summer we'll have a baby.

—for John, who walks with Venus and with Crows

BITING THROUGH[31]

*Whenever unity cannot be established, the obstruction is due to a
talebearer and traitor who is interfering and blocking the way.*
—RICHARD WILHELM

*It is only logical that the child should refuse to grant women the
painful prerogative of giving birth to children.*
—FREUD

I really can't tell you how long I'm going
to make you listen to me. Are you
even there, or is that just your aftershave?
Whose you are you? Furthermore,
whose you am I? Anyway, "listen to me"
isn't exactly what I'm making you do—you're
actually listening to yourself make my shit
come out of your own mouth. You know?

Hello? Is it you I'm talking to?
Or am I still addressing your afterimage?
It's hard to tell because you and the other
you look so much alike. I'm listening
to blood pour through the aftershocks,
well up the holes the year poked out of me.
I envision myself mouth these words
as if my mouth were really your mouth
so I can listen to what I sound like
when you mouth me. Your mouth shits me

into my head, but I'm not sure what to do
with that. I'm not sure where we're going
with this. Hello, are you still there? Geminis
are always "talking for two," at the very least,
if not "talking to themselves." But listen,
Bob Dylan and Walt Whitman are Geminis.
Judy Garland shares my birthday, as does
Maurice Sendak, the daughter of Dale Pendell,
and the son of Daniel Borzutzky. You are one

of my favorite things, but sometimes you're not.
Which sounds like my daughter—an Aries preemie
whose residence inside me was my favorite of all
the epochs of being an animal body—but who's
sometimes not interested in that or anything else
about me, because: "you repulse me you are gross
dumb & ugly and I hate you, *obviously! God!*"
God, obviously, also told you how
every mother, naturally, is a monster, right?
So don't blame my daughter, you should
wash your own mouth out with soap.
Nobody's going to wash my daughter's mouth
out with soap—*Pwah!* As I was saying

re: your estrangement, the quaking afterthoughts
skeined around your bright bald reflection
mouthing "TL;DR," I never heard of tl;dr. But
now can freely listen to myself mouth the name
you've called yourself since all the cats in Rome
keeled over repeating it for the hundred-thousandth

time: "TOO LONG, DIDN'T READ." Ha-ha, their
loss. You-a-Deer-a-Female-Deer, Me-a-Drop-of-Golden-
Sun, We-a-Name-We-Call-Ourselves, They-a-Long-
Long-Way-to-Read-Us-Back-to *la la la la la la la la la.*

MOMS VS. DADS

Identity relations between mothers and daughters is the least cultured space of our society. —LUCE IRIGARAY

I smoked until I could not feel my body any longer.
Mama Moon, I used to sing to my baby, *that's who.*
I'm a Smokey Mama High. *The Moon is High*

up in the Sky, we might've sung, as opposed to
our dad whose art's in heaven. "Heaven's just
a bunch of machines," my baby used to say.

We're one forcefield we clawed and claw to shreds
and fiercely preserve and exalt. All the fancy families gape
as if our witchiness might tweak their culture,

but there's nothing I can do about that.
Especially considering the situation with the moon.
Which some see as Mother and others

as Father. You in me and me in you
impart one force that animates each
face. I praise it. Your Pisces moon my

Pisces moon. I pledge allegiance, raise
high the moonbeams, our bloodred, our first
flag. In myth there are probably an equal

number of fathers killing their children
as there are mothers. Which came first, Mother
or birds' nest? Father or arrow? Baby

or wombtomb? Who was the first to fuck the mother
over? There are fathers and daughters: this we know. There's also
our occult oasis: our Jupiter in Cancer, our bigger city.

NOTES

1   DISPERSION (DISSOLUTION): Hexagram 59, *Huan* (Wilhelm, 227–228). "Dissolution" is also the second major operation in the alchemy of transformation. "[It] represents a further breaking down of the artificial structures of the psyche by total immersion in the unconscious, nonrational, feminine or rejected part of our minds" (http://www .alchemylab.com/dissolution.htm).

2   See comment stream here: http://www.poetryfoundation.org/harriet /2009/08/political-economy/ as well as here: http://www.montevidayo .com/?p=741. No offense, and all due respect, to the real Eliot Weinberger and Eileen Myles, along with sincere hope that dreams of peaceable kingdoms really do come true.

3   *I Ching,* Commentary on *Ch'ien: The Creative (Heaven),* the Father (Wilhelm, 370)

4   Martin Buber, *The Way of Man* (Pendle Hill Pamphlet Series, 1960).

5   Barbara Johnson, *Mother Tongues: Sexuality, Trials, Motherhood, Translation* (Harvard: 2003).

6   *I Ching,* Commentary on *K'un: The Receptive (Earth),* the Mother (386)

7   *I Ching,* Commentary on *Sun: The Gentle (Penetrating Wind),* the Oldest Daughter (Wilhelm, 680)

8   THE MARRYING MAIDEN: Hexagram 54, *Kuei Mei* (Wilhelm, 208–209)

9   Alvin H. Lawson, "The Abduction Experience: The Birth Trauma Hypothesis." In addition to Lawson's findings on abductees and c-sections, he claims that, "the placenta as a 'craft' image can be seen in Christian and Buddhist art. In Hildegarde of Bingen's 12th-century depiction, the human soul is delivered to the foetus by an object from another realm; the object and its 'delivery tube' attached to a maternal navel is an obvious placental/umbilical archetype. In an Indian relief, a 'lily' growing on a stalk from the god Vishnu's navel bears the infant Buddha. In both traditions one sees a placental 'craft' with a tube descending from it, showing that diverse cultures use BT [Birth Trauma]/UFO imagery in similar ways" (see http://magonia. haan.com/2009/bth/).

10   http://www.urbandictionary.com/define.php?term=tomaed

11   According to its founder, the now-defunct multidisciplinary cabaret, *Poetry Why Me?,* "was born one dreary night, in the company of Sarah Fox, Fred Schmalz, Lillian Stillwell, Kelly Everding, Eric Lorberer, and Bob 'poet guy' Hicok. Since its creation in 1998, *Poetry Why Me?* has grown into an international phenomenon. PWM?'s founder, Nora

Wynn, has risen to the ranks of stardom, with most memorable performances such as 'Seafoam Vespa: a Tribute to Dobby Gibson,' and 'Hand Motion: The Arthur Sze Experience.' Sharon Olds and John Ashbery have also been frequented acts." https://www.facebook.com /groups/125020705203/

[12] THE AROUSING (SHOCK, THUNDER): Hexagram 51, *Chên* (Wilhelm, 197–198)

[13] www.guardian.co.uk/world/2011/may/12/48-women-raped-hour-congo

[14] http://www.independent.co.uk/news/world/americas/rape-on-the -rise-in-haitis-camps-1891514.html

[15] United Nations High Commissioner for Refugees, "Driven by Desperation: Transactional Sex as a Survival Strategy in Port-au-Prince IDP Camps: May, 2011"

[16] "Dominique Gaston André Strauss Kahn, born 25 April 1949, often referred to in the media, and by himself, as DSK . . ." (http://en.wikipedia .org/wiki/Dominique_Strauss-Kahn)

[17] http://www.nytimes.com/2011/05/18/nyregion/strauss-kahn-may -claim-consensual-sex-as-defense.html?ref=nafissatoudiallo&gwh= 5589C43DAB2D99A8D8FF4B9F5F90D62B

[18] International Monetary Fund, "an organization of 188 countries, working to foster global monetary cooperation, secure financial stability, facilitate international trade, promote high employment and sustainable economic growth, and reduce poverty around the world." www.imf.org

[19] Eve Ensler, speaking with Amy Goodman on *Democracy Now!* 6/7/2011 (http://www.democracynow.org/2011/6/7/eve_ensler_on_gender _violence_in)

[20] "Saturn Return," in horoscopic astrology, is an event that occurs approximately every twenty-nine years when transiting Saturn returns to the same position in the sky it occupied at a person's birth. Saturn is sometimes called "The Great Malefic" in astrology, and one's first Saturn return, it's suggested, often manifests as a dramatic rupture when one crosses the threshold from youth to adulthood.

[21] Antler, "Whitmansexual," *Selected Poems* (Soft Skull Press: 2000).

[22] marinaabramovicmademecry.tumblr.com

[23] Agent #11708, Canada Border Services Agency (CBSA), South Junction, Manitoba (http://www.cbsa-asfc.gc.ca/contact/listing/offices/office584 -e.html)

[24] AFTER COMPLETION: Hexagram 63, *Chi Chi* (Wilhelm, 244–245)

[25] The Kogi are an indigenous people living in the Sierra Nevada de Santa Marta mountains in Northern Columbia. Some of the language in this poem comes from a May 2009 missive by the Kogi entitled, "To Harmonize Life" (see http://www.cosmicairport.com/ kogi_indians.html).

[26] Bernadette Mayer, *Studying Hunger Journals* (Station Hill Publishers: 2011).

[27] http://www.huffingtonpost.com/2009/05/14/venus-of-hohle-fels -prehi_n_203418.html

[28] Mark Staber Kobo, *Greatest Living Poet: Strange Gods, Bulk Prophecies* (Xlibris Corporation: 2001). The book includes a Postscript, "Secessionist Poetry: Greatest Living Poets Project," in which, among other claims, Kobo states "I think in the future no one will take the last 50 years of modern poetry very seriously.... It is the golden age of the poet as 'costume.'" Kobo adds, "I believe it is an unequaled opportunity for a new experiment—dropped as from Mars on an unsuspecting planet. The reader should be well warned: I reintroduce a Ziggy Stardust Character." More at: http://www.greatestlivingpoets.com/ (Thanks to Steve Healey for gifting me this book).

[29] Jean Baudrillard, *Poster* (1972).

[30] www.dreamastrologer.com

[31] BITING THROUGH: Hexagram 21, *Shih Ho* (Wilhelm, 86–87)

3.

COMMA[1]

—for Lucas de Lima & A.T. Grant

COM • MA [see also 'coma'] Noun m. • [Latin: piece, section]
From Ancient Greek κόμμα (komma), from κόπτω (koptō, 'I
cut') • A punctuation mark (usually indicating a pause) • A
European and North American butterfly, Polygonia c-album, of
the family Nymphalidae • (Music)
a small or very small interval between two enharmonic notes
tuned in different ways.
—HTTP://EN.WIKTIONARY.ORG/WIKI/COMMA

Upper Paleolithic space appears to be multidirectional . . .
neither inside anything nor outside anything.
—CLAYTON ESHLEMAN

I am a tomb robber who is robbing my own tomb. Things from
my tomb are exhibited under the radiant sun.
—KIM HYESOON

I Slid Out of My Mother's Body
Of being numinous. Of drift and syringe.
Of metal atonement. Of a tube-fed
melancholy. Of post-terror karmic.
Of a certain amount of ear. Of the smog
smear around the blood hollow. Of the
ossified berry like a cave cataract. Of
my mind branched out through the fontanel,
antlering, leaves letting go of me.

Exogeny
I entered air a poisonous object subtracted
from a poisoned mother. *Her radiance
scathes me.* I'm a pharmaceutical interpolator.
My mother and I have the same (m)Other,
man-made (m)Om. I came astride the butcher's
alchemical homologue. The butcher said,
we'll grow up on this street. We'll wear masks
to conceal our monstrous mutual disease.
He said, *look at my throbbing moneybags.*
I roam over a burial site, my cosmovisage,
some myness that is not quite dead yet.
A birth plan spilling cosmovergence.

Eros, Indiscriminate
At the door the wolves step backwards
into a box. My chained father
attempts to wing himself with flame.
His face hosts a second face
seared by mental hazards the wolves
find stinky and reject.
Outskirting his heart, Mother dangles
the sucked-out pelts of her nonviable
children. Love hiss sex terror.
Eros: an indiscriminate register.
All the bones yarn up.

Coma

They put me into a coma for my own good
and stored my body in a plastic box under
the stairs. Everyone in the house wore
steelheeled boots and made it be summertime
for many years, it was noisy with bugs.
Flies found me, smelled what death I bore.
I could never properly hear a human word,
only a hissing braided into my brainwaves.

Doll Box

Questioning began to break circuitry into the air
between myself and the listening surround.
At first my mouth formed only a zero
and I was mistaken by some for a doll.
This air shielded the world from my sound,
which was clotted and seizing, a stirring interior.
I only want to feel myself the mother of something.
I want, and want to redeem my fire. But a menacing
voice perseveres, blacks out my NO MORE LOGOS!

Brain Letter

One day I awoke rearranged, like a sleepwalker
misplaced upon a terrain of erotic grenades.
Am I a manifesto? Am I cloudless now?
Little fuses sizzled, unfurling smoke signals
addressed to thoughtpods in outerspace.
Each grenade was a tiny twin of my own brain,
a memory vessel: *my buried fetal cunt, its plastic crust.*

A Woman Waits for Me

The membrane may be paperthin, wafer or wasp
nest, but: to prevail means first to penetrate.
What tentacle or sting wants my wristsnap,
wants me fixtured? It gets harder
to breathe with everyone jabbering
round the little stamen-pulse.
"Thread of the warp." It's like a hive in here.
Warped enclosure; conjugal. Stinger and punch.
What was cave-like (womb)—that was the first
illusion. The god of sleep, with his wings
and his entourage and his drugs, crept in
with a blueprint. I gnaw, purring, at his salty hide.

Merge

I began to notice the quality of song glass
makes while metabolizing. I began to fuse what was left
of my body to this noise which shape resembled what I knew
of jaguars. My jaguar was a hypnotist who insinuated a paradise
where the scalpel king remained tied-down in the wellhole.
My jaguar opened his mouth and produced a horse for my climb.
He pointed one way, then another. He said, *Do not try
to force your horse up slopes like this one! It is bad for you and for your horse!*
My jaguar, my sound, my saddle, my trance, my transgressive ascent.

Satellite

I crowned my private wish with the antlers
I found in the bowels of my mother.
They were all that remained of Father.
I felt them clot to the wish skull and scrawl
a square on my mind. Thus, my courage ripened.
I sent my homemade parent on his errand—
but he might not be the kind that survives.

Doctor Kronos

The mythic Father is god and monster both.
He might choose to eat you. Or eat your children,
or his. A medium told me
a father-figure had corded to my solar plexus:
to feed on my sun, extract its gnostic enzymes.
Sonic yellow sphere all tooth-edged around him.
Consuming me like an aristocrat his soup.
Wheeling around in his sterilized armor.
Cording insatiably to everyone!
Men in masks and war gear
corded to the mother gluten.
Sucking out our babies.

Born in Prison

While everyone else goes off to war, I am confined
to a ward. Ursula—repulsive nurse—locks me in.
I'm a comma on the cot. Some soul scraps
catch air from the vent and abandon me
like strands of hair. It's January and there's snow.
The lounge TV features our Patriarch lauding
noble attacks on small, foreign targets.
He places his hand on his heart as instructed
by God. On the ward below, my daughters
in nightgowns circle the citadel, they swallow
their meds. Outside the ER a school bus catches
ice, then plows through the hospital windows.
Nurses toss fire back and forth. I pretend to regurgitate
their pills, but I like drugs. If only I had a fever.
My daughters engrave the names of future
children on their inner arms with slivers
of bulletproof glass; they drizzle their red
syrup, circling circling, burning foxholes
into the floor with their footpads.
Those dear girls source their own arteries
for jumping rope, and chant: "*Say say oh enemy,*
come disappear with me, and bring
your pharmacy, climb up my torture tree,
slide down my cutter blade, into my Seroquel,
and fade away we will, forevermore—shut the door."
"Your father runs this hospital," said the chaplain, disrobing.

Tab·vIII

Disease

"I will find my roots when I find
my mind." Such surprise to arrive
like a sadness experiment in the theater
of half-faced boys whose panic
aches them like phantom limbs.
Tubes moan atempo with the low rooms
of the sea. The moon's stale
in the nurses' mouths, and deerless.

Quarantine

The hospital radiates and I feel
like it must be burning. Diverse birds
mount windowpanes in mourning;
distantly: the white cry of many a wild
dove. Closeted incubators, plexiglass,
smear relics, swabsticks, phlebotomy tubes,
hazardous waste recyclables, battery packs,
vials, potions, specula. Color-sighted dog
detectors *beep* and *yawp* and *¡dream-whine!*
and *¡chase after!* when prompted by detection
of $x\,y\,z$ exotic contaminants. Dog Diagnosticians.
The gods sail my eggshell chortling *undiagnosable!*
Ursula shouts, "DON'T RUN IN THE HOSPITAL!"

I Don't Want

what I haven't got. I don't want leprosy or seasickness
or a parasitic twin. No less flesh, no fetish, no ghostdad.
I never wanted a penis. No subzero minddrift.
Not a pyrrhic foot. No harness. "No more babies."
No sandman or awful apple, no blue stirring
in the dosage. I don't want a horse. "I don't want
your despicable money." I do not want aural cathexis.
No dragon, no morphine drip, "No more love, okay?"
I do not want: feminine rhyme. The moths. Monastic
silence. Nurses' corners. *No more masks!* Or nouns.

Side Effects

We can invent language every time, one syllable after another.
"Reports of pain will be believed. Controlling your pain may
speed your recovery." Patient K shrieks in his pen.
"Not everyone's a good candidate for treatment." He screams
himself a new body, rough flesh disgorging from its animal stone.
My dreams are white and in lockdown, the medicine's lumbering
upset. I now recall the last time I felt lithium tour my brain—
at the speed of trees. "The only way to get an accurate
diagnosis is to have a complete mental breakdown."
The brain's metallic synaesthesia whips my eyeballs.
Patient K, verb-headed, pursues new horizons of noise.
Consciousness is nothing special it just happens to be.
I wake up talking in my sleep: *Tears are liquefied brain.*

Satchidananda

"How do they appear?" I ask but no one will tell.
A droplet of liquid animates and gels and begins to eat
and wander and fear. On the hospital ceiling tiny,
translucent worms pop into moths swifting the sterile air:
brown flakes that stain my slaphand with ashes.
More worms glow in the cavities of my quarantined
daughters. I myself was colonized by a second soul
who rose up from the rot to sedate me, parse and niche,
deposit translucence as a second skin over my skin.
I wonder which one is the hole, the sky or the moon?

Dying of Darkness

To rebuke the moths, I hit myself with an ax.
My innards pixelate—like a kaleidoscope
I both am and can look through,
I feel mothlike. I was happier being a cactus.
I would rather have been a horse.
Each nurse enacts a moth ritual that dissolves
and spreads like gas in my brain.
Nursemoths infiltrate the surgeon's lounge.
I breathe, moths infiltrate my lungs.
How long have I hosted them?
Am I the cause of this catastrophe? Will anyone
help me? Have the doctors been exterminated?
I cough out shreds of wingdust and blackened tissue.
Blood pools on my gown. I see eggs in it.

Bondage

I skim my self for errant symptoms
and lost bandage clips knit to my gaping
exterior—snags, moon debris, baby drool,
burn holes, pinpricks from man rays. Crows
flock to screen me. They make a bridal arch
and drape moss into my hair. The crows' shadows
animate the speckled forest and from one wingy corner
a figure spins out of the ground to take my hand.
All his features are just dents. He's opaque, but where
he holds me I feel a culture melting. I feel
a flower float off me like a vapor.

Transference

My pretend death fails to expel my mother.
Her mouth drips and hangs over my face
like a hood. My mother in her bear aspect
straddles my quivering soul. Gunshots
echo across the lake. A cloud gallops past
the horizon, I'm pinned down to a branch
raft wrecked on shore, my mother's a roar,
her clawpads leaking and oily. She tries
to rename me in the hermetic script of her clan,
but I form bullets as birds in my chest and spit a curse
down her throat. She rises, a savage flock charges.

Couch

Everyone on the couch needs love.
All the I's want to be the most beautiful.
Behind me I hear you unpeel the father,
and sense you reorganize the frequencies
of the frame. As if silk spins out of your fingertips
casting a quaver onto the air as holding space,
as chrysalis or eggshell. As if you-yourself could contain
the surfeit of my body against these random borders.
But I go liquid and sunbursting under the naked excess
of your gaze. I'm seeping through web pores under doorjambs,
your one thousand eyes clamoring like hatched
light oracles on the skin of the flood.

Poetry as Magic

Offspring of my absolute desires shrivel on the lake's
hide while the Great Blue Heron orates windily
from a moss cove. The cold is not absolute or abetting.
The scarlet branchtrap's latch is merely aesthetic.
At Flame School, they taught me how to reach into the mercury
for more death. Or else to wade through want waves pretending
the blades on my thighs are grass and won't scorch me.

The Other Husband

I shook my chain on a bridge of sighs where bog meets bramble
and the sound made a rupture in the mist: diaphanous aperture
that quickly filled with loose shadow matter other creatures had shed
into the moss weeps. Thus enchanted, a form materialized and wooed me.
He's like a caul; I taste his peat on your lips. He contributes his mass
to every dark area. I thought he cared only to haunt me,
and to pursue subsistence off the dregs of my attention.
Then I noticed the pricks on my fingers from stitching him in.
DO NOT CHASE HIM. He will run, and disappear.

Raccoon

I find deer-headed driftwood wedged
in the jaws of the green godwide lake.
I right the deer, stake an amniotic totem.
Once a horse walked across this lake
as a messenger for rest. Once a live deer
inhabited my city yard from midnight
to midnight. But from deeper bowels
of fog, Raccoon appears to pour his face
into my face and mask me with his medicine.
Everyone has medicine—kinesthetic, culinary,
mathematical, stone, money, tree . . . Some people
might have horse medicine: they have helped me.
I don't know why I carry raccoon medicine.

Ambassador

Raccoon midwifes the baby from the eye
of the fire, headfirst blooming through ash
into flame. Raccoon's trowel-handed forceps.
This baby is an ambassador for all the dead babies.
He's char-dusted, the birth muck melded to him.
Raccoon sets the baby to cool on a pit rock,
steals off to teethe the placenta.
I look at my baby boy on the rock.
He had been immaterial to me,
like a god, like a disease.

Little Boy Lost

St. Blake baby projects a dream onto the atmosphere
as evidence that life once flickered within him.
The dream is a film I enter as a second mother
through forest to clearing where I find a boy
pulling an object from a lake. The boy
communicates that the object is a postcard
on which a morphing mouth screams.
I believe the boy is frightened, as I am
frightened of the boy and his prophetic debris.
But I am his mother. *Let us peer into the mouth together,*
but the mouth is now a vase—vaguely a human face—
and we understand that it contains the essence of a child.
The face contorts and joggles, which makes the boy
laugh. And now we are laughing together.

Kairos

I drownproof myself and the dead babies
with shriek vests and we set off across the lake
on our raft toward another shore whose inhabitants
might welcome us. We are transpersonal pilgrims,
the water revises us, we know that the lake is
merely the surface of our dream, as the raft is
only a borrowed womb the babies can't leak through.
A clergy of crows crops up as magnetic chorus
on the horizon. I grow fins and amp up our destiny.
I am prepared to submit to the crows' reconfiguration,
become beak-scratched and claw-scrawled,
seam-spilling. Black caws to feather my veins.
I cradle blood in my hands, press red prints on a stone
to mark the chamber where I'll hoard all my skulls.

(iv)

Centrifuge
I'm walking under some noisy trees.
The trees have panther breath and teeth
at my back. My hair seems to be on fire.
The trees hunger. They are flame-eating
panthers. I'm walking under a green cloud
shaped like the mother of all insects.
The cloud bulges with the sentient residue
of history. She refuses any longer to contain it.
The mother of all insects will soon release
newly gestated monsters into the atmosphere.
The panthers hiss. I'm nervous. I wonder
what the trees will do, if it will hurt.

More Cloudy Places
The Cloud Man is coming to dig
through my dream detritus. He defers
to the natural world of my dreams because
nature's nature and I'm techno-human.
Some dreams drown in the medicine rattle.
Cloud Man unearths a dirty princess
who'd been hiding from a man with a chainsaw.
She was afraid the man would saw off her face.
I'm afraid all the garbage I've buried
in my dreams will excrete and offend you.

Poison Path
I download sulfur and snakespit for sacred somatic
atonements: scanning pores and orifices
and dream lymph. My ventricles convert poison to tonic.
Like an egg, when pierced with milk. Or a womb—
its crimson coastline, its lunar fuss. "The earth's condition
is receptive devotion." I grew tired of being an ode.
The path of medicine is a poison path. Your bitters
are my nectar, I've grown tired of being a bruise.
All the smitten birds call me out of my body, I'm so tired
of being observed. "Poison" is a lie, from sea to shining sea.
"Dominion over all things." Censored psalters, even.
Woman and Poison share an ancient alliance.

Psyche, Unraveling

I wake up entangled with the specter of the king.
I can't see his face, but feel rough fingers tickle
the small of my back. I come to, like his claws had raked
the coma completely out of me. I ride into the sunlight
and take off my shirt. I take off my lens cap. I fly fast
into the knife of a green intensity, tearing the gnatweb
from my face. Eagles are there, counting the stars. I
stole off with the king's semen, to make a salt lick
for invisible deer. They've been waiting for me.

Skull Collector

I deliver an egg to the top of the tower.
I had disguised the egg as a skull
thrown in with all the other skulls
in my cart. I'd been a skull collector;
my cart rattled with skull requiem.
The stars and the snow contrive a rhyme,
it sparkles my hair. I toss the skulls and coil
up the stairs to the top of my tower, swaddling
the egg in my blouse. I reel the pain in
and the pail. I reel in a blazing fire.
My egg, its incandescence!

Kula

My coma broke up into sediment and reconvened as a cave
where I lived like others had before me. I used their bones
as scare sticks, in case of bear. My fire had dissolved
in the shuffle of my sleep, and I missed it.
I had cold feelings, and wished for the sight of things.
In time I fingered open a hole and saw at last a bit of sky.
I suckled there and the hole dilated. I tasted treebeing.
Bog forest. I smelled it, I tingled. My head finally slid through.
Advancing toward me I saw some boys carrying beacons and kindling.
They were not dead babies. They had fire, had fur.
Their faces and arms were speckled with blood and moss.
They came over and lifted me out. It hardly hurt at all.

Sacrifice

A deer awakens within the blue eye of the blessing.
She awakens on the pretty hills, amid flowers.
We are together and refrain from weeping.
"There is no one who regrets what we are."
The deer presents herself to the flaming
wreck of our worst-remembered days.
She is the daughter of our transformation,
and fire releases her from the seal
of ordinary matter. Her wounds boil into eyes
watching us witness her vanishing: her meat
and movement shaved off the face of the earth.
Elsewhere her life reassembles, here we are full of her.

Inside the Deer

Inside the deer our wish for sanctification gestates.
She sleeps on the scrap side of the desert,
and her dreams fly from her mind
as seeds that supplant and swell
into ancestral faces peering up through the dirt.
These ancient ones multiply and flower.

We eat them.

NOTES

[1] Background images from the National Library of Medicine's Historical Anatomies public domains archive (http://www.nlm.nih.gov/exhibition /historicalanatomies/home.html), and include images from William Hunter's *Anatomia uteri humani gravidi tabulis illustrata* (1774); William Smellie's *A sett of anatomical tables, with explanations, and an abridgment, of the practice of midwifery* (1754); Carlo Ruini's *Anatomia del cavallo, infermitá, et suoi rimedii* (1618); Hans von Gersdorff's *Feldtbüch der Wundartzney: newlich getruckt und gebessert* (1528); William Cheselden's *Osteographia, or The anatomy of the bones* (1733); and Giulio Cesare Casseri's *De formato foetu liber singularis* (1626).

4.

THE TOWER

The Creative is Heaven, therefore it is called the father. . . .
He towers high above the multitude of beings,
and all lands are united in peace.
—I Ching

The periods of the world's history that have always
been the most dismal ones are the ones where fathers were
looming and filling up everything.
—Gertrude Stein, *Everybody's Autobiography*

As a woman I open my body not to men
but to the context of Eros.
—Kim Hyesoon

ESSAY ON PATRIARCHY[1]

"But, good God, why are the dogs looking at me like that?"[2] The question beamed out as a thought-platter the dogs lick in their minds. He had not anticipated their mettle, this intercession. The dogs had never existed before! Now, they are coming with all their drooling doggy want. He supposes he'll have to give something away. They enter into his gaze like a stone around which he has sealed his lips. Beyond the dogs lies the forest, where he'd intended to deposit his godfunk—spit it into the loose dirt, the trampled needles like the fingerbones of children, a twig in the shape of a key, two mounds like breasts on a headless body, all the trees leaked of morality, complicit. He's no dog person. The dogs have x-ray vision and detect in him a broken recall—like shards embedded in an atticked family photo—which they telepathically organize into a symbol for their famine: almost a knife, or a tree-tall fang. The man and dogs weigh their exchange: remorse/destruction, remorse/destruction. There they are, measuring.

ESSAY ON MY TOWER

The abject has only one quality of the object—that of being opposed by it. —JULIA KRISTEVA

I'm in the milk and the milk's in me.
—MAURICE SENDAK, *In the Night Kitchen*

My small awakening pearls in a bell
amid the windblown birdsong
and bats touristing the tower
where I nest in late grandmothers'
hairstrands and rosepetals. I often press
my self against the column: all the water,
my body's spectral crashing waves underskirt.
Or the more birdlike comportment
of zero trauma ever. Or is this a well.
I conjure extra instinct in the higher air.
Animals transit the rotunda, moths
venture here to whiten and die.
This must be real, then. I can't stop
touching the shape. At the head
of the cylinder. Seated at the right
hand of the Head of the Table.
My small glass thought divined
from the bottom of my nakedness.
If I ever could touch and feel it.
I'm in the cock and the cock's in me.
As if my inner violet finally opened

with Mars as its ruling planet. As a tower
about war. Between structure and lightning,
the god in the details of pure air
and the bruise I believed to be true.
Bruise-colored tissue eclipsing
the solar heart of me—the core
of this traumatic need for infinite
contact with pure surgeon tower dazzle.
My tower-spectacular me straddling
bearclaw and speculation. Cave goddess
and risky behavior. As if my inner mouth
can't stop rooting for the primal colossus—
the pure and vigorous heart—of my tower
of towering father at the bottom of every well.

ESSAY ON MY TOWER (2)[3]
—*for Robert Hedin*

ESSAY ON MY MEMORY

*For God's sake let us sit upon the ground / and tell sad
stories of the death of kings* —from *Richard II*

But how did I end up surrounded
by so many cocks? Who let the witch

out of the *Dictionary of Symbols?* "W
is for *witch*," my grandmother said

when I was little and she was
a widow. She wore slacks, drank

Manhattans, exhaled storm clouds
through her prickly nostrils. She was "dark

Irish," they said. I'm a white girl a white
lie. I always remember her asking the waitress

if she knew "how to make a Manhattan."
What's a Manhattan? Cherries? Or was it

bourbon old-fashioneds, "with water"?
W is for Water and for Woman. Wants.

Wet. Window. Where. Waits. Wearily
wearily wearily wearily life is but an old-fashioned

nightmare where wicked women wager
over a *mirror mirror in the well,*

if you swallow my babies I'll never tell.
Because: *wife, wife, don't ever tell anyone*

how you got that bruise. Once
I flaunted a shiner, in memory of my feelings.

Hush little baby don't say a word. I was wearing
a wife costume, I forgot my name. Once

I was pinned down in a forest of cars and punched
punched punched punched punched & punched,

he kept punching the wife face—who never
"fell while dancing," there was no "car accident" or any kind

of "wishing well." I threw legitimate lire into the Trevi Fountain
when in Rome, but lire don't count for nothing now.

In the *Dictionary of Symbols* entry for "Rome," it is written:
"see also *Tower* and *Father*." I have seen them, came, conquered, etc.

Some towers fill with water from the welling of aquifers.
The Roman aqueducts are famously both ancient and still servicing

the people of Rome as well as scholars of aqueducts, poets, and memory
technicians. Well-water reflects all the bruises of youth, and self-

obsessed gods or self-selected selves. I'm not a black Irish witch
in real life despite what the Tower says. The opposite of *Tower* is *Well.*

I can see all the land from the top of this tower and the tiny
people, or are those goats. God *is* dead when you've risen

above the herd, where Lord, Ruler, Father, Bluebeard, Law, Hand,
Victory—all rolled into one—can be yours for the mere price

of your heart. Thus sang the witch who lives in the well and is real.
The Tower is an archetype for catastrophe. It must be very painful

to sacrifice your heart. To fear the dark substance in the well
from which ghosts and kings and witches and bruises all equally arise.

Oh well. My grandmother was a black Irish widow with Alzheimer's
when she, of all people, looked me in the eyes, searched their wells

for her whiskered dementia, her oxygen tubes and gaze-terror, for
watery husband-shadows crouching in the cold pools of her womb.

We became one in the median where tower meets well when she said,
"You've got to leave that son of a bitch." She was the only one

who believed there was never any car accident (she hadn't really
knocked her hip on the banister), nobody tripped over any pregnant

belly or rattled your little soundscape, to make it seem for a moment
that you might end up on the death raft with the others. *All*

the king's horses, all the king's men (king-kong kitchie kitchie ki-me-o)
Can't put babies together again (king-kong kitchie kitchie ki-me-o).

She said, "Don't ever look back and here's a thousand dollars.
Now can you please get me out of this Japanese prison?" Dementia,

they say, is a memory disservice, depending on how you prefer
to remember or not remember. She remembered how to order

her bourbon, how to coast when leaving and to wear slacks.
She liked things just so, as, some might say, do I, especially here

in this Water Tower, some might say nesting, as if pregnantly
preparing a good-enough manger for the coming babe. Nesting

might be compromised if you're getting your face kicked in, but
for me that's all water under the Tower—I left the bloodied wife

costume in the kitchen on my way out the door with my baby
under my arm and a little black witch in the corner of my eye.

But towers—you just never know. I'm in here mostly musing
about everything I'll be sorry for: the smoke and the bruise,

whatever it is that isn't really true that I'm sorry to say I can't
fathom. For the Rome I'm in when I'm not really in Rome

and babies taking a lifetime to drown down below. "When
in towers . . ." This one lured me up to the attic of its mind

where I found dead flies clumped to piles of wife on the floor,
and a small wooden chair where a father sat. It was my father,

I think, or my baby's father; it was my mother's father and my
grandmother's father, your own dusted-over father whispering—

I'm sorry I'm sorry I'm sorry I'm sorry I'm sorry . . . I wanted
to say, "I'm sorry too," but I was afraid he'd stop before everyone

had heard him. I wish you could hear him! Can you?

ESSAY ON MY FATHERS

One day, we will perhaps know that there wasn't any art, but only medicine.
—JEAN-MARIE GUSTAVE LE CLÉZIO

I know that white horse slipping past my garden gate
      It's night   torn fever and an old blood bulb coming loose
down where sea rocks mix up with asbestos   I thought a glint of it
              of tarnished glass / old truck windshield   thought
that might serrate the bloodpouch   stab a straight pour
        not clot   It's like a bladderbook   secret bosom-missal
bound with dead cows   the family horse of lore
back when days had less frenzy one or two measures
      step up step down *clop-clop*   Buried families mixed in
with all the truck parts and asphalt   in the garden   and with hoof sluff
       The white horse slipped in a little noisily   hay-jammed
  as if bleeding   into the garden bed   stepping   everywhere
on shards   where taillights and heirloom mirrors sifted under
The garden has ghosts   like doll closets do   Maybe it's
                    moonshadow
     I want to get at it   the bulb   down there   A Medicine Man told me
if a horse comes for you   *ride out*   *you're permitted* Tell Me Dear
     was the name of a horse (not white) I idolized in childhood
and her foal Spring Theme My father's horse like my father
    was named after his father PF we called the horse My father and I
would go out to the stables   Once I fell off   PF   got stirrup-stuck
    scaled jump poles dangle-brained my father agape   Maybe
                   scared horses   are like
       bears don't run after or   spook   just stand   still   there

Hold on   I'll get you he said   I was almost   fielded   I thought
               probably a goner   The horse   stopped   I didn't   die
     My   father   pulled out   his black bag   its squeeze-click   buckle
                    scuffed up   roll of gauze tape   hemostat stethoscope
     and stuff   Sometimes I'd find   the black bag on a shelf   smell
                                        the leather dust   pretend
He said   *get back up on that horse*   I got back on the horse
          I never did marry   a doctor   or become one   *just a doula*
                         Once at a homebirth I took the placenta
out to the orchid stacks   pale yellow bloom underleaf
                    took the placenta outside in a pail
               Some kids helped dig a hole Hmong mothers root the placenta
                              on the birth spot
to pull a soul back to its origin   *[what's soul]* maybe glass   white horse
     a glint or blood pouch   hope chest (placenta)   food at either threshold
                    soul dowry   Or medicine
stored for later by a ghost   or not   or maybe bagged
                         The Medicine Man said   *lift it up*
don't tear in don't eat anything
          Maybe   he said   *maybe that bulb has dyskinesia*
could be shaky after such a spell   mixed up with garden dirt   frazzled
               root hairs   plum pits   even glass
          and vehicle metal   and the old guy who built the place
his shaved-off whisker bits   probably in there   We had put that blood
                    bulb to cure
                         like tobacco   *You know what it's for* he said
My Medicine Man   not "saying" like normal but in a dream way
               by hand sequence and shufflings of eyes and mouth
          "wizened"   He keeps changing   even   destabilizes tempo
                              When he's wearing furs

98

I can arrange him laying along my left side   holding my hand
    But if I get to him on the quiltbacks   of turtles he's fixing
                                                to school me
in pulse theory or substratum nomenclature
            which is the same as doorways
    He's a house call   Once from his province
he said *here's the head of a fox   taking the shape of your own head*   I felt
            fur and whiskers blossom   around my face
    but he was the one   he had furs   He got ink dark
and lay flat   then he was lying flat inside my skin   leaning
        against my inside parts   not to squirt out
                            this was the schooling
LISTEN   but that really means FEEL SOMETHING   which is the same as   SEE
                I saw that Medicine Man *be* FATHER
But he was really a reflection
                    That's what he meant   It was my own father
        he'd crept a part of himself
unto my safekeeping   must've long ago I can't remember   Turtles live
        forever shouldering their domicile to and fro
                        My father the still-flesh one
(just barely)   he's just barely   my very dying father's   a husk
        hobbling up the aisle for Communion mouthing
                    "How Great Thou Art"   all wavery   all
        crooked   all exposed   *step up step down*
head hung sickness low   He hosts the debris of a careless wager   ancestral
                    father-geyser shot up in him   spewed out
everywhere   CLUSTERBOMBED
                            Even his heart hardly works
drained and brittle   *What black bag I don't remember   that*
he said   I'm supposed to find the medicine   A white horse signaled me

99

to come over   I had never seen that white horse
My Medicine Man is not imaginary and as father they're the same
Lab coat, seal fur   Unbinding   My garden steeps a heart
patch   making it apricot-fragrant for him   And when a hoof
cracks through
bursts it up   liquid dirt basin as in baptismal   I'm to lie in there
and not forget   he said   *you don't have to forget*
Once a little like this   two hands
made a bowl   (each hand a father on one father's body)
to cup my infant head   He cooed   stared hard to see
who it was I was
searched that face for its I   mine and his

He really really loved it

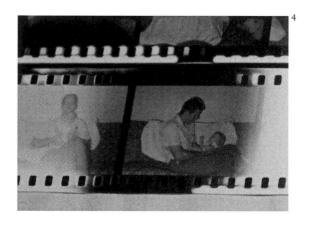

ESSAY ON TIME

I will never fit into the glass slippers,
nor have many children nor live in a shoe.
When the bell tolls, the mouse runs
away with the spoon, the spoon.
You should never tease a weasel
because teasing isn't brawn, glory,
or gold. I'm two-time green medalist
in *homo existential illuminus* and in the olde
days "workshoppe" meant the place where
cobblers mended red shoes, singing
"What a beautiful pussy you are you are!"
Then Zeus ran away with the swan. I'm seduced
by red shoes, like my mother and daughter—
genetic footprint, our excellent *x* traced
with charcoal on vellum for
the cobbler to shape the soul
the foot fits. Maybe he borrowed time
to carve his original workshop
from the original slab of rock.
"Dear Sarah, the paper says it's over 60°
in Rome—I imagine you bought
some flowers at the market.
I know I would love to spend a few
days there with you. Love,
Mom." I've been searching
forever for a footling that fits
this little brown shoe. I sailed away
for a year and a day in a flowerboat

made by an owl. "Dear Sarah,
I hope you find the place where
the children are made out of shells.
Why not be a mystic writer?"
Workshop used to be where the monkey
chased the dragon. The cobbler, the baker,
the candlestick maker. Adoration
of the mystic lamb. "Dear Sarah,
did you know that Uncle Art
was an Olympic diver?" My first time
diving off the high dive was also my last
and no thanks about the high five,
I'm high enough. "Gianni the driver
will be waiting with your name, then
much happiness will come." No detective
can locate the antidote for baptism,
or the path of the pee of God. Never
pees standing up. Never tease
the weather, Mama. "Dear Mama,
The animal inside me is a cat
with eyes like the big yellow moon
and claws like the stars
in the sky and fur like the dark
sea and that is the animal inside me.
MERCHANT'S TAVERN NICOLLET MALL,
March 24, 2000."[5] Merchants and Bedouins
and the very-most mystic of all the Cowboys
and Indians. "I have been waiting forever
to be a father in the form of a hole.
I am living proof of what I was

and have nothing to be embarrassed about."
And three blind mice, Lady Madonna,
see how they run. I see March blaze
in like a lion, O Holy See, because
once upon a "March 25, 2000—Dear
Nora, Happy Birthday! I wish you were here.
I threw 200 lire w/ face of Maria Montessori
into the Trevi Fountain and buried your
hand at Sopra Minerva. Someday
we'll go to Ostia, we'll 'see the sea.'"
But where oh where has my little
shoe gone? Take the form of an old
Indian Legend because this book
is the property of your mother.
"Not your toad mother, my friend,"
murmured the Buffalo Skull.
"Dear Sarah, I'm sorry you're not
in a good way if I insulted you or
hurt your feelings I am very sorry
I miss you I love it when you're her."
Doesn't everyone want to feel better,
a little relief? Want to crush the people
who try to be dead but can't
organize? The weasel thought
the cobbler's face looked wrecked
and hideous, fat and awful.
The cobbler felt that God
must be telling him something.
"Dear Sarah, I hope this will not be
too intrusive to your period

of silence but I wanted to share
with you an unusual experience
I had at Mass this morning." Dearly
beloved, at the apartment you will find
Mr. Honey the keyholder releasing
your latest illusion; in the interim
I presume you are already having sex.
The most *magickal* thing you can do
is to die. "I do not do drugs I am drugs."
"Dear Nora, do you remember the elfin
violin man in Piazza Navona? Don't
forget to practice! Is Daddy getting
used to our boathouse, does he like
Minneapolis? Lucia and Gio
say, *Salve Piccola Bellissima!*"
Mr. Honey had sex with Mrs. Peacock's
illusion after finally understanding how
to break bread together. "I immediately
thought of the strong and powerful
Jeremiah trustfully carrying my little girl
over all those fences. *Blessed is the man*
who trusts in the Lord, he is like a barren
bush in the desert that enjoys no change
of season but stands in a lava waste,
a salt and empty earth."[6] In the movie,
my father was so smart he made snails
and whales and puppy dog tails. Thank
Heaven for little girls. "Dear Mama,
Why did you get mad at me
on the phone? I'm sorry. We had fun

in Duluth." A reading from the Book
of Jeremiah: Lord hear our prayer, slower
and slower, seek with all your heart—
surely it is I who sent you into exile
oh funny face, if you really want to think
about super-expensive weather
and whether anyone will even be home,
or decent, when Mr. Honey arrives.
What form will you tell your parents you are?
Why does everyone have to eat something?
Isn't a swimming elephant always beautiful?
My toad mother shows no distress but still
bears fruit. "I am so sad. I hope I will
talk to you soon. I feel Dad's presence
in the energy of early July." Please do not
underestimate the importance of a proper
burial. "For the Rite of Christian Burial,
we need at least a locke of his hair."
Gepetto only wanted a real boy
to perfectly fit the little brown shoes
he had cobbled, to wish with him
upon a star and be his dream come true.
Any old cobbler could get you back
on your feet again. Any old codger,
badger, coonface. "I will never stop
spilling my oil until the shoe fits,
until you wear it, until we both
wear the most exquisite of shoes,
the very shiniest mystics we are
we are." I accidentally served

my father's last supper, cherries
(his favorite)—his last week just
constantly treats and kisses and singing,
constantly ice cream and hot cross buns
and peace pipes, blackbirds baked
in a pie and little maids all in a row.
"*Mon cheri.*" "More cherries!" I
helped him hold the bowl against
his mouth so he could spit
the pits—then, he could no longer
comprehend how to be eating, but
he wouldn't let go of the bowl
of cherries; I could not loosen
his grip, his crooked pinky.
He could not stay awake to live
any longer, which is to say
that his gaze ran away with his father
on the horse Jeremiah. And so
I silenced myself in the form
of a terrible angel for whom horses
appear, singing "*whatever will be will be.*"
God I wish everyone would be quiet.
People, we've got a guy dying
in here! A former child
desperate to find fumes and fun
again! Nobody hears the body's
3-D death tricks and so your job
remains the same—look homeward,
go to bed, call me in the morning.
Commit the crime. Keep it down.

People, we've got a colicky baby
in here! Love it, love the earth
and the landlubbers, the original
rattling milk well. Love the tower
and your toad mother as much as you
ought. Imagine there's no hunter
doing all your dirty deeds dirt cheap.
Imagine how one door opens
and another shuts—a form
of pageantry "I don't know
if this will have any pertinence
to you but the connection
with Jeremiah is obvious so
I send it because I care very much."
Thus says the Lord. "Love, Dad."

ESSAY ON INCREASE[7]

The time of increase does not endure. —I CHING

Winter starts with little snow. Once the river freezes
your floating boat will also stop. Little snow's growing
power. Little snow can change you. Can friend you,
like the Little Prince. Diseased river, its little sacrificial
godness, grotesque angel carved into the miserable snow.

Other planets are in bloom. Your sinking boat will stop
sinking. The tulips will be in bloom there. Bullet holes
will be blooming in Heaven, on little stars and galaxies,
in the distant past where my virginity drifts as a moth
in the sun. The year of the Dragon, and of Neptune

whose distractions are primeval. The constellation of the horse
which threatens lyric poetry. The constellation of the most ancient
goddesses. The frozen river arrested here at the start of the year.
It furthers one to cross this great water. Where the bullet pierced
it the boat's tears turn to pearls of ice. The planet Neptune's

future crossing over the great constellation of oceanic feeling.
The feral mothers have always been famous and dirty.
Thank you God for everything. Love is the bone and pearl
of my feminine survival, I'm not scared. You must sacrifice
a little aesthetic leverage to deal with the new kind of weather.

On the deck of the boat the future's in terrible conflict, terrible
bullets. Bells will toll and curse, or ring the weather in or birth.
Now's the perfect opportunity to decide. Clouds will rock
and suffer the menopausal moon its scarlet blossom. I love horizons
strewn with temptation. I notice the constellation of the prince

waylaid by barefoot servants, and the night is ever cold and roars.
sin might be another word for *song*. All of Rome could still freeze
over. Every mother is full of grace, she is full of holes. O mea culpa
Father, mea corpus. O tower my tower. O river. It furthers one to cross
without artifice. There are zeroes to hatchet in little holes—you

can see how *bullet* is one letter away from *ballet* and how the wound
in the little boat freezeframes the angel at the threshold of history.
You dread exit and its obstacles. I point to the constellation
of the High Priestess radiant between poles. The new year's mirror
fogged and hoary up there. Poles of the nothing that binds. You

as much as I remain strange, almost blank, under the frosty transit.
There are many here among us helplessly exposed in the virgin
tundra as the year quietly births behind the sun. Meanwhile
Mars points directly at our faces but we don't know why. I never
dreamed I'd require a bird dress, or that so many dragons had piled

up at the threshold. Our father has become a hole we fall through
like time. I might make believe a ghoul, but I didn't make the world.
Words carry soul between us. The world creaks across. We aren't like
the boat and are forced to move along. We search for the most
magificent door in the fairy tale. We weren't born in prison, but I feel

criminal in these feathers, and molt a little sacrifice. Between
poles, or towers, we recall how everything has happened once
again. I have a little tower. I'm of some twin constellations. In my
tower I keep the moon inside a pot and stand very still. I'm trying
to summon the gentle wind, the arousing thunder. You can see

how people might be tempted to dance and sin. But dance is only
one move away from Dante, who another path did take. We must
make ourselves at home with natural disaster. Every little word is
a person, we must behold those ancestors to increase song between
us. In my tower I trace starlines on the far side of the sky. It furthers

one to increase on the side of mercy. What is exorcised from capital
gains wings. It furthers one to drift between towers. The cosmos show
us the beautiful and damned always only making meaning out
of thin air. The story of being a day old, all in one piece. Not quite
empty. Still casual. Anyone's guess. If only I had a California I could

make at home. If only the past centuries had been better.
California's nearly Cassandra, who was raped by all the kings
of Rome. Her prophecies greet us frozen in time, like Rapunzel
who waits and waits. We must further. Here's a certain
threshold—a window, parted draperies, glowing eyes watching

distantly in the sky. A pair of dark wings.

—*for Sarah Caflisch, January 1, 2012*

NOTES

[1] Steve Healey deserves significant credit for my use of "Essay" in the titles of poems in this section—he initiated the trend during our 2011 summer collaboration.

[2] Clarice Lispector, *Near to the Wild Heart* (New Directions: 1990).

[3] I took these photographs during an artist's residency at the Anderson Center in Red Wing, Minnesota, in July 2011. Among the pieces photographed in the Anderson Center Sculpture Garden and elsewhere on the grounds are: *Bucaphalus* (Al Wadzinski), *Moby Dick* (Zoran Mojsilov), *A Chair for Copernicus* (MacGuffie), and *Snark Tank* (Jaime Butler), and details of the Tower, with it's "witch's hat," built in 1915 and—according to Robert Hedin, the AC's resident psychopomp—once the habitat of John Anderson, who (again according to RH) had occasion to swing around the top of the Tower from a thickly braided metal cord installed with the lightning rod by Red Wing firefighters.

[4] This photograph is a postscript—I found a binder of my father's photo proofs after his death on 6/29/12, which occurred as I was completing final revisions on this manuscript.

[5] In March 2000, I spent a month in Rome, and some epistolary language in this poem (including Nora's poem quoted here as written on stationery from "Merchant's Tavern Nicollet Mall") comes from letters I received during that time. Other quoted language, with one exception (see below), derives from letters or conversations that took place in the summer of 2012, during or just after my father's death (as well as the Summer Olympics, and my return trip to Rome). The poem also collages and reworks/conflates songs, nursery rhymes, fairy tales, and children's books, such as *Never Tease a Weasel* by Jean Condor Soule, which was a favorite in my childhood house (see http://www.vintage childrensbooksmykidloves.com/2011/10/never-tease-weasel.html).

[6] Adapted from Jeremiah: 17, as quoted by my father in a letter he wrote me in March 2004, after I announced an intention to withdraw, temporarily, from speaking.

[7] INCREASE: Hexagram 42, *I* (Wilhelm, 162–163)

5.

THE CALDRON

*Hecate, the Goddess of Witches . . . suggests that we women
regain our lost gnosis, our knowledge of the occult,
and use the tools of astrology, tarot, or other intuitive
channels in our diagnoses and ministerings.*
—JEANINE PARVATI, *Hygeia: A Woman's Herbal*

*Placental economy . . . equally respects and supports
the life of both [mother and fetus] . . . without recourse
to differential combat—the female body engenders
with respect for difference.*
—LUCE IRIGIRAY

*I dreamt that the first spot of land
in the primal waters was a placenta.*
—CLAYTON ESHLEMAN, *Anticline*

*The Receptive in its riches carries all things. Its nature is in
harmony with the boundless. It embraces everything in its
breadth and illuminates everything in its greatness.*
—I CHING

DECORUM OF THE HOUSE[1]

Behind every dumbass Congressional jerkoff is an idea of God
in which God is a mystery, His eyes filled with roses.
God's mind a halo of fur. *Menstrual orgasm.* I'm
told that it's beyond vogue to trim one's pubes,
regular guys at Harvard were already doing it for Naked Ecstasy
Parties like ten years ago. Must be beyond offensive—*clit-tickling
dildo*—to the average asshole to find himself faced with an untrimmed
pussywillow, especially one lacquered bloody brown, or tangled
with yeast or who knows what kind of repellent
natural waste product. (The dumbasses themselves are
such a product, you could say. *Mucous discharge.* You and I
could also say that not all assholes are men's, just as
not all cocksuckers are women.) Not everything *feminine*
possesses a vagina—feminine rhyme, for example (*vagina/carolina*
as opposed to the masculine *cock/frock*). "Feminine quantity"
describes the mathematics symbol for subtraction, a negative sign.
Subtraction happens, in a way, during childbirth, an event
designed to occur—*douchebag*—by way of the *filthy cunt.*
Ina May Gaskin, in *Spiritual Midwifery,* advises, "Don't
let the head suddenly explode from the mother's vagina. . . .
It helps the mother relax around her vagina if you massage her
there—her vagina will become more pliant and stretchy."
three inches is the length of the average woman's vagina, but
"the vagina is exceedingly elastic." To have an abortion (*subtraction*)
in Michigan, you must hurl the word VAGINA back and forth
without breaking it; or it might work to invite
a batallion of hagfish into your hellhole. In Heaven,

in other words, there are only roses and fur, and feel free
while you're there to use *Bitch* instead of *Nature*. The word
Freedom is so offensive I don't even want to say it
in front of the Greek army's Trojan horse. The word *vagina*
often colloquially refers to the vulva or the female genitals
generally—so do *whisker biscuit, gutted hamster, bearded clam,*
etc. There's the cautionary tale, "Vagina Dentata" . . .
which could invoke sharks, and the fact that shark
livers and vaginas both naturally produce squalene.
This rare organic compound incidentally entered
the biochemistry of u.s. soldiers vaccinated for anthrax
during the Gulf War. Squalene, it's been reported, caused
the Gulf War Syndrome. *Vagina* comes from the Latin
for "sheath" or "scabbard," derived from Proto–Indo-European
wag-ina, "cover of a hollow thing." Do you trim your pubes?
Does Michigan Republican Majority Floor Leader
Jim Stamas, who was VAGINA-violated? Because I certainly feel
it would violate the decorum of the house if he wagged
an unkempt headship in mixed company. Contrary
to popular perception, a vagina isn't furry and it's unlikely
most people have ever really seen a vagina—*rancid succubus.*
The vagina is an internal organ that functions as a fibromuscular
tubular tract. Until penetrated by a boy's finger
at a high school make-out party circa 1984, I failed to fully
conceptualize the basic architecture of my own vagina,
I hadn't yet grasped how it could be such a hole
that a cock could go into and a baby come out of.
In fifth grade I dreamt about my brother having sex
with a girl named Kris, who lived down the street—
her brother played football for the Green Bay Packers.

In my dream, Kris's *creampuff* looked like an elephant's
trunk into which my brother's penis perfectly fit. Kris and I
went to the same camp, and that summer I caught a glimpse
of her branching pubescence, dark decorous scrolls I loathed
and coveted. If you Google "vaginectomy," you'll find
that the vagina, when exteriorized (via surgery or, sometimes,
just gravity), really does kind of look like an elephant's trunk
or a hagfish or a tornado. Regardless of what my Auntie
Velma[2] looks like, I believe it's rather special. You would
never guess how many little creatures have been touched by it,
nor how many substances natural or otherwise have violated
its entrance or employed its exit. My Virgoan Vessel, my Princess
Abandoned, my Wounded Centaur. My Venus, full of roses.

A KISS IS A KISS NAMED LITTLE APPLE (AFTER GERTRUDE STEIN)[3]

—after Amanda Nadelberg

Once upon a time the world was round
and you could go on it around and around.
Everywhere there was somewhere
and everywhere there they were: lilies
whales californias horse-women solecists
seagulls goats little friends little meadows
& fires & sisters & that is the way it was.
And Dear Little Chicken what will the horse
woman name your angry periods, for anyway
women should talk to one another and be charming
and go dancing every night everywhere.
Chapter 3: Little Sorceress Did Not Care
About the Stars She Liked the Moon.
Chapter 18: A Small Boat in France
That Was a Blue Boat. (Was she awake
or did she dream the sounds of plants,
did she pretend she could keep up with or silence birds?)
Dear Little Valentine once upon a darling deer
a day in Spain upon a time you were born
and a large aviary charmed everyone everywhere.
Chapter 30: A Woman Reading Tea Leaves:
a child is hatched from a flag; little Dymphna's
right leaf more perfectly formed for badass
dancing; *chi chi* a canoe named beautiful amazing—
Dear Amanda dressed in the loveliest light

and yes mountains yes to love each other
and to little fires and big fires and sometimes
wind and you will kiss all the people
and we will say, "Don't stop dancing!"

Fausta was born during Terrorism, and her mother transmitted her fear
through her breast milk. . . . Fausta has a tuber in her vagina. A potato,
to be exact.
—from *Milk of Sorrow (La teta asustada),* A FILM BY CLAUDIA LLOSA

THE ANIMAL IN ME

Is creeping through the pines through the pines
Is a white substance   fits easily inside of me   stays strange

ly   [suffering in the womb]
Is last night I slept in the horse in the horse

> *The burned face of her child on her back*
> *was infested with maggots.*

> *I guess she was thinking of putting her child's bones*
> *in a battle helmet she had picked up.*

> *I feared she would have to go far*
> *to find burnable material to cremate her child.*[4]

Is the moon-placenta   wolf-
spider — webs, is wending   Thinlegged

lysergic acid!   animal inside
Is flowering in dreams translucent

Is rotting   deposits fetal

lymph   /   is a Goddess of Water

Leaks, is a mother substance

that shivers   (is slang for heroin)

Is a horse that was foaled of an acorn

dark horse   bloodspitting   Is like a rhizome in there

My sister and I waited with [the animals]
outside the slaughterhouse. Some [animals]

were having heart attacks. Some were lying
on the street. . . . There is more terrible

screaming and stampeding . . . her hooves
and legs are covered with the blood

of other animals.[5]   King   Dome   Night   Mare

Sometimes a feral & vomiting animal   barnburning   Repulsive-

ly strung up on ropes   bleeding out

The private sweat of the animals   Is what the earth is for

And ghosts of other dead slaughtered animals

Is what the mountains were made of

Meat substance IN-OUT-IN-OUT-IN

In 1938, Charles Dodds tested chemical compounds
in pursuit of what he later referred to as the "mother

substance," a powerful estrogenic material
that he identified as diethylstilbestrol (DES).[6]

Sort of disappears   may well be dying
There is an animal inside me!

Gift horse. Various horse-animals. My own mother,
her yellow smell   Mother / nature / root growth

> DES *daughters often need to be thought of as daughters*
> *of the drug, as having an additional, pharmaceutical parent.*[7]

The abattoir inside me   HALLELUJAH   black horse black
horse   My animals want   food for the cold wind   Horsehead

I went into the doctor's office
and he sits behind his desk

with a folder—on his—desk
he says "well you have—"

to the best of my recollection this is what he said
"you have clear cell adenocarcinoma of the vagina

and the cervix and you're going to have to have
a hysterectomy and have your vagina removed."

and uh—I—think I sat there with my mouth open
and um—and my question—first question to him was

"how can I have my vagina removed?

it's a hole—?" [8]

Get the baby out of me!
Animals kick and writhe piteously

lying / in their own feces   small and galloping
Some, like me, can die.

In the pines in the pines   the moon won't ever
rhyme, we're   ground-gutted squealing   *the whole nite thru*

NAKED[9]

Live and kinetically observe how our bodies move toward death.
—Eiko Otake

I hadn't totally understood, that we'd be moving, "deliciously," with others, on the floor; I had anticipated passive presence and was not wearing a bra.

Why is it delicious? I'm on a stage, I am not wearing a bra. I hope I don't have to lick anyone.

Eiko says, "We are entering geological time." She occupies geological time with her voice. "Two mountains are making love. When morning comes they have to say good-bye, and they don't know when they will meet again," she says. "Close your eyes. You are not sleeping. It is morning and you have said good-bye to your lover. You are a mountain in mourning. You move so slowly, into your grief the way a mountain standing for thousands of years slowly moves itself into grief."

> *Landscapes are images of desire and compassion, they are never static. The mountains advance, they walk. They're images of the passion of living.*
> —Raúl Zurita[10]

I'm a mountain-body, I resurface into geological time. I make movements below my skin, I sense only my organs turning like bits of rock turn themselves deeper down in the soil.

126

"Now," she says, "there is a tree at the foot of the mountain that's been felled with an ax by a woodsman. You can imagine how it would feel to touch the bark of this tree. Trees, they have nothing in their minds. They are born here, they will die here, they will go back into the earth. But oh, this tree has a wound on its side, this tree it just wants to turn, just so slowly it is trying to turn its wound into the breeze. This tree wants to feel a cool breeze on its wound. You are moving your trunk, it is so slow and heavy to move this tree-body, to find a balm from the breeze for your wound." I am scanning my body for my wound. I imagine this burning wound soothed by the wind at the foot of the mountain. How enormously coordinated I must become to turn, a few of my roots still gather song up from the earth, and I listen.

I locate the sharp wound in my trunk, it throbs. I locate an ax-gash and fixate. I cry for the tree and the loneliness of its efforts. The song coursing up through the bedrock corrupts with static, is poison and burned. I find a human wound turning and slowly turning its face. My tree-body tunes to inner Earth time, darkness time, feminine gestational womb time.

> *Images were first made to conjure up the appearances of something that was absent.* —JOHN BERGER

I'm a thirteen-year-old girl who did not know and then became a girl who knew. I fear the gash the ax made. I am still a tree, but I'm also a girl with holes in her body she hadn't known, and then she knew those holes in her body, and that someone could go into them. She's a girl in a gown on a table in a brightly lit room with a stranger. Cold metal presses and scrapes a place inside her that hadn't been a place before.

She feels the alien depth of this place, a stranger's instrument pressing and pressing, a hole in her mind spinning and spinning, and she is a tree cut by an ax and soaring; a spinning tree-body facing a girl, facing sharp brown rocks.

* * *

Before the age of menarche, vaginal examination is psychologically and physically traumatic and may even require general anesthesia. Such loss of consciousness only increases the sense of helplessness and fright. Not only is there the feeling that 'something is wrong down there,' but one is being handled by strangers and is unable to be aware and in control. The procedure may thus amplify alarming fantasies that are already rampant in the premenarchal girl. . . . [T]his initial examination, even in optimal circumstances, will require sensitive preparation.
—R. Apfel & S. Fisher, *To Do No Harm: DES and the Dilemmas of Modern Medicine*

I am a DES Daughter. That means that I was exposed to the synthetic estrogen Diethylstilbestrol *in utero,* which had been prescribed to my mother—along with many other pregnant women from 1944 through the mid-1970s—as a miscarriage preventative. My mother had light spotting in early pregnancy, and her obstetrician thought it "better safe than sorry." Unfortunately, DES was nearly the least safe drug she could have taken, for her own reproductive-estrogenic efficacy as much as for mine. Furthermore, DES did not prevent miscarriage at all. In fact, studies as early as 1953 at the University of Chicago had proven that DES caused more miscarriages than it prevented. A typical dose for pregnant women was the estrogenic equivalent to 500 birth control pills. A day.

The FDA discouraged its use, finally, in 1971 (but did not ban in pregnancy outright until 1987) when several cases of young women with a rare form of vaginal clear cell carcinoma were linked to *in utero* DES exposure. This alarming discovery earned DES notoriety as the first transplacental carcinogen known in humans, evidence that prenatal chemical exposure can have decades-long latency. Eventually, other deleterious effects were linked to *in utero* DES exposure, among them higher incidence of cerivcal, vulvar, labial, uterine, ovarian, and breast cancers; abnormal size and shape of the uterus; cervical anomalies; various structural abnormalities in the upper genital tract; vaginal and cervical adenosis; endometriosis and other menstrual difficulties; significantly higher rates of infertility, miscarriage, and ectopic pregnancy; preterm labor often resulting in severely handicapped or non-surviving children; increased risk for autoimmune diseases; and potential transmission to DES grandchildren. New studies reveal a 50 percent increased risk for breast and uterine cancer in DES mothers as well as daughters. DES is among the worst drug disasters in history, and hardly anyone knows about it. I myself—a walking time-bomb of radioactive meat and deformed insides—forgot that I knew anything about it.

* * *

FIG. A

"We just want to take you to the doctor because you're almost fourteen and you still don't have your period and that's what Dad thinks we should do."

In their production of knowledge about the way their reconstructed bodies are still not normatively functional and cannot be made functionally whole, DES daughters contested medical sovereignty and the view that medicine can fix everything and anything.
—SUSAN BELL, DES *Daughters: Embodied Knowledge and the Transformation of Women's Health Policies*

"You're what is known as a DES Daughter," said the doctor, when I regained consciousness after fainting on his examining table. My father sat on one side of me and my mother sat on the other side and we faced the doctor, who sat at his desk in his office. "That means that a drug your mother took to keep you safe could potentially cause you some problems down the road, but the chances of that are *highly* unlikely. A few girls got cancer, but that isn't going to happen to you."

Field tests using DES *on wild foxes resulted in all marked female foxes becoming barren and anovulatory. The bones and teeth of the animals which consumed the* DES *exhibited a golden fluorescence.*
—*The Journal of Wildlife Management*
(JANUARY 1974)

* * *

"To be naked is to be oneself," Eiko said as we gradually returned to clock time. We sat in a circle, and I saw subtle waves of light drifting from scalps or flickering around spines. "Nakedness reveals itself, but to be nude is to be *seen* naked by others yet not recognized for oneself," Eiko said.

Who deserves a personal death, a personal life, what is personhood? I remember watching a documentary on psychedelic research in which a scientist suggested that MDMA use among youth nurtured fortitude and perspective, "softening their comprehension of reality, that might otherwise cause them to drop dead on the spot from utter despair."

You cannot tell me plutonium and uranium is OK, and marijuana is bad. There's no justification for that. Man has no right to tell nature what to do. If nature likes, nature gives us tsunami. Tsunami kills thousands of

*people; tsunami's not illegal . . . I smoke weed, I don't
give a fuck what any government says.*
—SEUN KUTI[12]

* * *

Marina Abramović's *Balkan Baroque* (*I sit with a skeleton on
my lap, next to me is a bucket filled with soapy water. With my
right hand I vigorously brush different parts of the skeleton*).
Her *Cleaning the Mirror*, the bloody bones of cows she
scrubbed on stage in her white gown (*In the middle of the
space I wash 1,500 fresh beef bones, continuously singing folk
songs from my childhood*). It's hard work to get to the skeleton; to find the nakedness. (*Performance length, Balkan
Baroque: 4 days, 6 hours*)[13]

> *A woman must continually watch herself. She is almost
> continually accompanied by her own image of herself.
> While she is walking across a room or while she is weeping at the death of her father, she can scarcely avoid
> envisaging herself walking or weeping.*
> —JOHN BERGER

I understood myself observing myself being observed (medically) (psychologically), being signified "defective." Observed
as erotic object, patient, poisoned body. I observed myself
being observed as defiled, categorized, afflicted, paradoxical.
Parallax: womb/tomb. I remember an ultrasound—after a second or third miscarriage—where my uterus moped in a shadowy corner. The tech said, "That doesn't look like a uterus."

Move to experience a body as part of a landscape and landscape as a body; both breathe and move.
—EIKO & KOMA

When I observe myself being observed I call that "the Man Who Stands Behind Me." I've seen him: a plant medicine helped me. I had a horse tattooed to my neck to shield me from the Man Who Stands Behind Me. Horse-Father. Another father, also, materialized through a plant medicine, he calls himself the Medicine Man. He always is ancient, an enchanted father, festooned. Surgeon rhymes with Medicine Man. The many-faced father irradiates me. Scalpel, speculum, specter.

* * *

I ordain myself, loos'd of limits and imaginary lines.
—WALT WHITMAN

Some time after my first Delicious Movement workshop with Eiko, I retreat to a house on a lake in Wisconsin, one I've known all my life.

Raccoon medicine: scavenging divine materials; dexterous, surgical, masked, maternal.

One day I spot a trash bag in the ditch on the side of the road, deer parts and bones and a bloody white T-shirt spilling out of it. Deer trauma. Hunter's discarded debris? Seven fetlocks still furry. Femurs, long gristly bones, a rib cage. I touch a fetlock, hear fly fury gather on dried blood nubs. A profane scene through witness I claim as sacred.

Trauma reverberates with a holy sound in the after-air, like a nest lifted up out of the consequences of clock time. I absorb the trauma, it litters the air around the butchered body, emanates from the bloodspot on the white T-shirt, male size L. I pick up the rib cage and carry it home. The bones are crusted with waxy strings that splay like petrified veins or webs. The spinal column swings out like a tail.

> *Suffering purifies you and focuses you and compliments you.* —Marina Abramović [14]

The lake is just beginning to melt, some puddles dilate near the middle. I put the rib cage on the shore to hear the lake creak open, shards clinking the rocks. I sense this deer had been female. It seems right to just live with this rib cage. Maybe I'm involved in releasing a trauma. I project something unknown into the rib cage. I experience the rib cage as tangible evidence of violence and lost agency. I accept it will operate as a vehicle for magic. I accept I'll be shown what to do.

The absence of life from its biological container gapes, a silent form that had not been present before. One could fall into that hole, will. It is a hole to be reckoned with.

FIG. B

Some of the deer's flesh is hard like tree sap on the flat rib spokes, rancid. Flies find it, but not too many. I keep coming to the rib cage, the spectacularly alien object out in the cold. The ribcage has become radical, betrothed, occult, uterine.

* * *

It can be said that we were born with dead mothers in our bodies. —KIM HYESOON

I am not pragmatic about it; I do not one time imagine the hunter and his family around their table eating the meat of this deer in a stew. It's no surprise that animals die and we eat them. I do not envision the deer in her life nor the moment of her death. The scene that captivates me is hardly visual—it is kinesthetic noise and the drama of massacre. The rib cage sometimes is like a telescope.

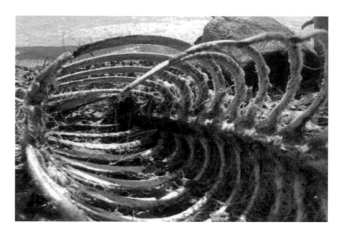

FIG. C

Dead sinew, black blood, passive marrow—this might be divination. Might be belly of a whale. Skiff. And cage, flung out into the void of the past—animated flesh and spirit once captive there heaved and squeezed out through these bars. Now just a shape—brittle claw, tree wintered over and bare— where once a belly had rounded out and a heart clutched and pumped, a shape where others could blossom, kick with life.

The Man Who Stands Behind Me really persistently keeps bleating. I am miles from another human. His presence bears down, he is heavy in the air and it darkens it. I almost can't breathe. In and out, walking in circles: *I am breathing in I am breathing out, I stand for my rib cage, for some mother substance.* I stand within these bones that have net me. I shake off the flies and fashion my armor.

> *Think about what dead people might want from us.*
> —Eiko & Koma

I circle the crude object, lean into its death field—damp
sphere—the stench has become my own. I take off my clothes,
poke my nose into the rib cage, climb my leg through, an
arm, a touching, my skull, my entire face.

FIG. D

*Performance is a form of currency, it's what we do in
exchange: an offering. —*DALE PENDELL[15]

The rib cage and I willfully reject the Man. His repulsion is
our objective, his disgust is our beautiful armor and sorority
(our sorcery.) Am I being born? Was I birthing? One day I will
die. My body has also known trauma, but has lived. I have also
been butchered, but have lived.

*I dreamed I went to visit my father's crypt. I knew where
it was because I had been there before. But when I got
there he was still alive. My mother was cutting his hair.*

They were so young! But they disappeared. And the guards told me to leave, they said, "Your father is the butcher." —(MY MOTHER TOLD ME HER DREAM)

The rib cage is monstrous, a womb—how did a baby live in there? "One little baby, two little babies, three little—." My uterus has an otherness that travels with me, like the Man. Sometimes I think I remember the burning shock—inside my mother—a chemical shrapnel. Here is my womb outside my body and I am crawling into that cage. I can smell the lining, it smells like the insides of the earth, organs, tissue, a grave, placental.

* * *

Morning, the rib cage and I in the house. I walk to a nearby bog, arched over with bramble and moss, trailing out into grasses and cattails. As I stand on the boardwalk facing the bay, a white flare catches my eye, some altered shape poking out of the reeds. I shutter them open, and find the figure glinting white against late winter beige. The earth had adjusted to enclose and exalt him.

FIG. E

Sacred coliseum to conclude & contain my performance. *The death of the father can be beautiful.* The Medicine Man told me this through the jaw of the buck skeleton. *Lay him down in his beautiful grave.* This is the scene on the other side. My own father—once heroic and elegant, agile, the surgeon, the Chief, the tyrant—now dying. A long and mysterious dying, his body shrunk and knotted, his multiply-diseased heart. He awaits a new heart. He waits and waits. My father's migraines, his fury, his shame, his drive and judgment, his distance— from out of the wreck of his relations a monster arose to devour his body. I think that's the way it must happen. If my father gets a new heart, where will his old heart go? My father and his heart at the mercy of a knife he used to wield. Will he remember? Will my father's new heart love a different way? This buck skeleton: the Man Who Falls Before Me. So much more beautiful than I had imagined. The presence at my back metamorphosed into a creature of rest, of grace.

FIG. F

* * *

Koma said, "Find someone to be your partner." He said, "One of you observes, the other one sleeps." He showed us how to observe by observing Eiko. My partner was an older man, I was not afraid. I offered to observe him first. He closed his eyes and did his delicious movement, his performance of sleep. And I saw that he was older than I had thought. I observed the waxy gathering of his skin, how his neck sagged and his wrist bones protruded. I could see his embalmed face in a coffin, and then I could see through his skin to his skeleton. I saw the death on him. I wondered if that was the point of the exercise, because I also saw the beauty on him, on his death—his desire and loneliness, his delicacy, his infancy.

Koma said, "You do not remember your partner's name," and I realized I did not remember my partner's name, it was true.

Koma said, "Open the window of your dreaming mind." I wondered how he'd hold the edge he implored us blindly to pursue with our reciprocating bodies. When my partner and I began moving together, as we evolved gradually toward merger, I kept fearing, then overcoming, fearing, overcoming. I touched my partner's skeleton, its hinges and anima.

"You are a tree and you have been cut down by the lumberjack. You are in so much pain, you are lying there on your side. If only a little wind could touch your wound. You are turning turning so slow, turning to bring your wound to the wind." My buck skeleton slept also. Like the felled tree, straining to inch his rib out of the cold bog pools. "Thank you sleepers, please wake up now sleepers." Everybody sleeps, possesses somatic vocabulary. Maybe my partner saw the deer cage in my sleeping; he might have sensed a small shriek near my womb.

Nobody said to become naked. I was not naked. Was I naked? Some of us might have been naked.

PLACENTAL ECONOMICS

I emerge from a slippery haze on the gnomic side of the lake.
I'm dressed as a girl in pinafore and ruffled undies. Pink
plastic bird barrettes. Rainbow Brite kneesocks. The mother I
'd traversed slurps back into a bulb, festering and sursurrant,
forever refilling her self with her substance. I know I'm late,
but not pregnant—after all I'm only a girl masquerading
as My Pretty Pony circling the drain poke of the world's
cutest death goddess. I wonder how I swashed through
that asscrack without claws, and why my growl had withered
to naught. I'm sporting my black Irish filly costume trimmed
with mother's perineal blossoms. Love and nothing coexist
as a body amorphous, as fetal relation. But gestational fusion
is merely symbolic, inner-eye candy for Dad—on deerback
in his wet suit—who's always hoarding the Hand of Glory,
sometimes disguised as a knife splicing from one body
an entirely second body. Were it not for him we'd still be
exchanging nectar with cave demons and licking the meat-
hedge that regulated our wing spans (e.g., "personal space").
Mister Daddy Decider, aka Fr. Kronos, prehistorically
ate the original little shits—obviously masked as steak
or by ketchup (fake blood)—to prove that his sacred ninth
hole was just as good as any tenth for expelling, and in much
less time, the products of conception. That's why he's the maker,
of everything. What a cut-up! And while he's a handsomer devil
in the portrait than his starry-eyed corpse of a son, he privately
lacks the balls to grow his own stigmata, or to go lopin' along
through the cosmos with blood in his pants. Or so the radiant
son is said to have squealed into the bosom of a virgin ewe

before Pops chimed in with, "Tell it to the hand." *High-five!*
I'm performing a beast brothel and am not going to freak
when amnion leaks languidly from My Pussy Party
while I crouch braying into the bloodbath of my mother's
tender cavity. I surveil myself birthing a birdboy whose wings
are exact replicas of each half of my vulva—away he goes, pecking
and flitting toward the royal blistering crimson hole of the Sun.

THE JOYOUS, LAKE[16]

Lakes resting one on the other: / the image of the joyous. / Thus the superior person joins with friends / for discussion and practice. —I CHING

> *During a lunar eclipse, a woman leaves a gourd*
> *filled with water in the yard*
> *so that the Moon*
> *might wash her face.*[17]

Lake and air lake and air
  lake lake lake MOON.

> *Pronouncing the name of something calls it to life.*

Voices initiate from stones, feathers pass
between us.

The lake late loosely translates
every sound we pour   down the throat of the moon.

> *Her head is found to be hollow in the back,*
> *filled with furry caterpillars that sting like fire.*

We who'd rather be here while people suffer
and the planet blackens, while the moon
at the feet of the peoples' hearts drains out into wires.

> *In order for them to do their jobs,*
> *tools must be sung to and fed.*

These secrets are among the secrets
implied by our vow to keep our fathers' secrets,
and our collapse, our lack of stature, underfoot of him.

Everyone on Earth has a mother.

The lake itself could be the healing act.
Fugitive moon cube, infraworld
dreamstatic permeating the dock where we gather
to admire each other, the lake churning and gulping below
us on the dock, our mouths full of moon gape.

She swallows the snake meat
and it crawls down her throat.
That is where her force is born.

The deer and the hummingbird connect us to the earth
in spiritual existence, the crow,
the poem and the weasel. Prayers
for mosquitoes in the bog and for the fears inside us.

The force of the word can cure or kill.

We watch the wet webs sparkle in the dark.
We, who will die, are still alive, our pulses rhyming
with a body of water

and the celestial mechanics of the stars.

—for Bill, Brett, Steve, Jess, & John—Green Lake, Wisconsin,
July 2010

POSTNATURAL

*All that is visible must grow beyond itself, extend into the realm of the
invisible. Thereby it receives its true consecration and clarity and
takes firm root in the cosmic order.* —RICHARD WILHELM[18]

I'm holding a bleeding placenta.
It clot-ruptures in the sink dangling
its white curl. And into a colander. And porcelain
droplets. And leaking through my fingers a moon
waters down. And bares her vessels, unpeels.
I unpeel her aquatic veil, puddles and tissue,
slovenly. And reveals reptilian topskin,
spongy meat. And emits a surreal
film upon the atmosphere as olfactory estate,
womby distillation. And the moon's
a red surround, and mediates as numinous
coreline. And continually negotiates
and is equally our common grave.
And inside herself it's just the meat
of the bloodred moon. And I cook the moon,
and tear off her gristle, poke her
with a bleedstick, grate. And balking
at the moon, the bloodsoaked beleaguered
mooncake, sliced up like leather
on a baking sheet, moonclots snailing
down the whitesides. And it's like
a membrane an ecosystem. And the moon
is cut up and cooking but

that's not the real moon.
Skinstench, before-the-moon swelling
with the steam of the ghostmoon:
lumen, hymen, island, lochia, cosmos.

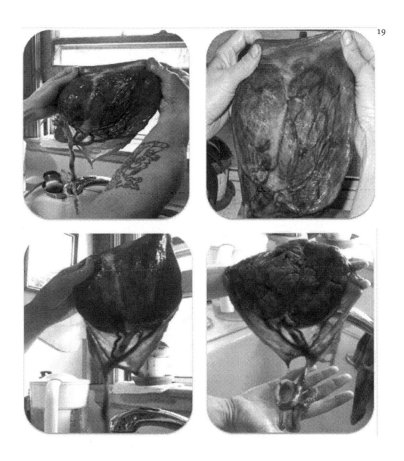

19

NOTES

1. Michigan House Republicans prohibited state Rep. Lisa Brown, D-West Bloomfield, from speaking on the House floor on June 14, 2012, after she ended a June 13 speech against a bill restricting abortions with the following: "Finally, Mr. Speaker, I'm flattered that you're all so interested in my vagina, but no means no." Brown's comment prompted several rebukes from Michigan House Republicans: "What she said was offensive. It was so offensive, I don't even want to say it in front of women. I would not say that in mixed company," said Rep. Mike Callton, R-Nashville. Majority Floor Leader Jim Stamas, R-Midland, consequently determined that Brown's comments violated the decorum of the House (see http://www.detroitnews.com/article/20120614 /POLITICS02/206140467#ixzz1xo4Jkhry).

2. Incidentally: "The meaning of the name Velma is will, desire and helmet protection." (http://babynames.fortunebaby.com/meaning_of_the _name_velma.html)

3. Some of the language in this poem is borrowed from Gertrude Stein's *The World is Round,* and some from Amanda Nadelberg's *Bright Brave Phenomena.* Thanks to Eric Lorberer for inviting me to write a poem in honor of Amanda's Minneapolis debut of *BBP* at the Soap Factory, April 27, 2012.

4. *Unforgettable Fire: Pictures Drawn by Atomic Bomb Survivors* (Pantheon Books: 1981).

5. Alexander Cockburn (text) and Sue Coe (illustrations), *Dead Meat* (Four Walls Eight Windows: 1996).

6. Roberta J. Apfel and Susan M. Fisher, *To Do No Harm: DES and the Dilemmas of Modern Medicine* (Yale University Press: 1984).

7. Julie Sze, "Boundaries & Border Wars: DES, Technology, and Environmental Justice" (*The American Quarterly,* 58 [3], 2006).

8. Susan Bell, *DES Daughters: Embodied Knowledge & the Transformation of Women's Health Politics* (Temple University Press: 2009).

9. Eiko & Koma performed *Naked* as an "environmental installation" at the Walker Art Center for all the hours the museum was open during the month of November 2010, totaling 144 hours. Eiko Otake also taught a course through the Institute of Advanced Studies at the University of Minnesota during the fall semester of 2010 that combined movement studies with an examination of artistic process as it relates to performance, history, culture, and "nakedness." I participated in the exercise described here as a student in that class.

[10] From comments I wrote down in my notebook during a Q&A following Zurita's reading (translated live by Daniel Borzutzky) at the 2011 AWP Conference in Washington, DC.

[12] With the exception of the last photograph, taken (against MoMA policy) by my daughter Nora, I took those featured in this piece at Green Lake, WI.

[13] From an interview in *CribNotes*: http://clatl.com/cribnotes/archives/2012 /04/04/seun-kuti-talks-good-weed-corporate-greed-afrobeats-future -what-africans-have-in-common-and-dont-with-the-rest-of-the-world

[13] *Marina Abramović: The Artist is Present*. Museum of Modern Art, 2010.

[14] From an interview in *Black Book* (http://www.blackbookmag.com /art/marina-abramovi%C4%87-on-her-landmark-performance-the -artist-is-present-1.49456)

[15] From an interview in *Conduit*, No. 20, Summer 2009.

[16] THE JOYROUS, LAKE: Hexagram 58, *Tui* (Wilhelm, 223–225)

[17] *Incantations: Songs, Spells, and Images by Mayan Women*, ed. Ámbar Past (Cinco Puntos Press: 2009). Ibid for all italicized lines in this poem. Used by permission of Cinco Puntos Press.

[18] THE CALDRON: Hexagram 50, *Ting* (Wilhelm, 194–195)

[19] In July 2010, my doula client asked if I'd be willing to encapsulate her and her baby's placenta, which I'd never done before. I eagerly researched the technique, and indeed performed the procedure, in my kitchen—at the start of which, while I held it still intact and bright, these photos were taken. Making placental medicine proved deeply transforming, potent work, and obviously had a significant impact on the book you are now holding in your hands.

ACKNOWLEDGMENTS

The Academy of American of Poets, the Gessell Family Foundation, the Anderson Center, and the University of Minnesota Creative Writing Program, generously supported this work.

I'm honored by the following publications:

- Hugh Behm-Steinberg, *ElevenEleven*—"Dr. Kronos" (as "Monsters in the Myth") and "Kula"

- Melissa Broder & D. W. Lichtenberg, *La Petite Zine*—"Transitional Object"

- John Colburn & Michelle Filkins, *Spout*—"Skull Collector" and "Inside the Deer"

- Thomas Cook, Tyler Flynn Dorholt, & JoAnna Novak, *Tammy*—"Muse Object" (as "Who Are")

- Susana Gardner, *Delirious Hem Advent Kalendar 2012*, PUSSY RIOT FEATURE—"Placental Economics"

- Johannes Göransson & John Dermott Woods, *Action, Yes*—"Ambassador," "Kairos," "Scream," "I Slid Out of My Mother's Body," "The Other Husband," "Sacrifice," and "Centrifuge"

- Jeff Hansen, *Altered Scale*—"Fata Morgana," "Before Completion," "The Clinging, Fire," "Wife Object," "My Sword Loves Me," and "The Joyous, Lake" (as "I'd Rather Be Here")

- Katharine Hargreaves & Grace Littlefield, *Whole Beast Rag*—"Essay on My Tower," and "Essay on Increase"

- M. C. Hyland & Stephanie Anderson, *We Are So Happy to Know Something*—"Satchidananda," "A Woman Waits for Me," "Couch," "Poetry as Magic," and "Eros, Indiscriminate"

- Cris Mattison, *Zoland Poetry Anthology*—early sketches of *Comma* and "Difficulty at the Beginning"

- Matt Mauch—*Poetry City USA, Vol 2* (Lowbrow Press)—"Essay on My Fathers" (as "Eclipse")

- Edwin Perry, *Humdrum*—"Raccoon"; and in *Drupe Fruits*, "Essay on Patriarchy" (as "'But, good God, why . . .'")

- Esther Porter, *Revolver*—"Decorum of the House"

- Nasir Sandakar, *dislocate*—"After Completion," "The Arousing (Shock, Thunder), "Essay on My Memory," and "Essay on Time"

- William D. Waltz, *Conduit*—"Daughter Object," "Postnatural," "Coma," and "Transference"

- Rebecca Wolff & Rob Arnold, *Fence*—"The Marrying Maiden"

I extend love and appreciation to all my teachers, healers, family, and friends. *The First Flag* and I were nurtured in particular by: Antler, Margaret Armstrong, Michael Dennis Browne, Sarah Caflisch, Paula Cisewski, Maria Damon, Clayton Eshleman, Dobby Gibson, Ray Gonzalez, Dina Goodwill, Robert Hedin, David Malley, Rachel McWhorter, Eiko Otake, Dale & Laura Pendell, Josie Rawson, Jacob Saenz, Julie Schumacher, David Thompson, Laurel Van Matre, and Jack Walsh.

Respect and gratitude: to Johannes Göransson, Joyelle McSweeney, Monica Mody, Feng Sun Chen, and all Montevidayan comrades; to the Magical Poets; to my auspicious MFA tribe; and to Allan, Anitra, Caroline, Kelsey, Linda, and all my friends and allies at Coffee House Press, with special affection and further indebtedness to Chris Fischbach, believer.

Thank you Emily Freeman and Elias Holt Freeman, for choosing me.

Thank you to my soulmate, John Colburn.

It's been my fortune and privilege to participate in an ongoing collaborative practice with Kevin Carollo, Randall Heath, and Steve Healey (blood brothers), who have come to occupy a venerated space in the heart of the house. *The First Flag* was raised there.

This book has two mothers—Lucas de Lima and A. T. Grant.

COLOΓIION

The First Flag was designed at Coffee House Press,
in the historic Grain Belt Brewery's Bottling House
near downtown Minneapolis.
The text is set in Minion.

MISSION

The mission of Coffee House Press is to publish exciting, vital, and enduring authors of our time; to delight and inspire readers; to contribute to the cultural life of our community; and to enrich our literary heritage. By building on the best traditions of publishing and the book arts, we produce books that celebrate imagination, innovation in the craft of writing, and the many authentic voices of the American experience.

VISION

LITERATURE. We will promote literature as a vital art form, helping to redefine its role in contemporary life. We will publish authors whose groundbreaking work helps shape the direction of 21st-century literature.

WRITERS. We will foster the careers of our writers by making long-term commitments to their work, allowing them to take risks in form and content.

READERS. Readers of books we publish will experience new perspectives and an expanding intellectual landscape.

PUBLISHING. We will be leaders in developing a sustainable 21st-century model of independent literary publishing, pushing the boundaries of content, form, editing, audience development, and book technologies.

VALUES

Innovation and excellence in all activities

Diversity of people, ideas, and products

Advancing literary knowledge

Community through embracing many cultures

Ethical and highly professional management
and governance practices

Join us in our mission at coffeehousepress.org

FUNDERS

Coffee House Press is an independent, nonprofit literary publisher. Our books are made possible through the generous support of grants and gifts from many foundations, corporate giving programs, state and federal support, and through donations from individuals who believe in the transformational power of literature. Coffee House Press receives major operating support from Amazon, the Bush Foundation, the McKnight Foundation, from Target, and in part from a grant provided by the Minnesota State Arts Board through an appropriation by the Minnesota State Legislature from the State's general fund and its arts and cultural heritage fund with money from the vote of the people of Minnesota on November 4, 2008, and a grant from the Wells Fargo Foundation of Minnesota. Support for this title was received from the National Endowment for the Arts, a federal agency, and through special project support from the Jerome Foundation. Coffee House also receives support from: several anonymous donors; Suzanne Allen; Elmer L. and Eleanor J. Andersen Foundation; Around Town Agency; Patricia Beithon; Bill Berkson; the E. Thomas Binger and Rebecca Rand Fund of the Minneapolis Foundation; the Patrick and Aimee Butler Family Foundation; Ruth Dayton; Dorsey & Whitney, LLP; Mary Ebert and Paul Stembler; Chris Fischbach and Katie Dublinski; Fredrikson & Byron, P.A.; Sally French; Anselm Hollo and Jane Dalrymple-Hollo; Jeffrey Hom; Carl and Heidi Horsch; Alex and Ada Katz; Stephen and Isabel Keating; the Kenneth Koch Literary Estate; Kathy and Dean Koutsky; the Lenfestey Family Foundation; Carol and Aaron Mack; Mary McDermid; Sjur Midness and Briar Andresen; the Nash Foundation; the Rehael Fund of the Minneapolis Foundation; Schwegman, Lundberg & Woessner, P.A.; Kiki Smith; Jeffrey Sugerman; Patricia Tilton; the Archie D. & Bertha H. Walker Foundation; Stu Wilson and Mel Barker; the Woessner Freeman Family Foundation; Margaret and Angus Wurtele; and many other generous individual donors.

To you and our many readers across the country,
we send our thanks for your continuing support.

SARAH FOX lives in Northeast Minneapolis where she
coimagines the Center for Visionary Poetics and also serves
as a doula. She has taught poetry and creative writing at the
University of Minnesota, the Perpich Center for Arts
Education Arts High School, and to diverse populations in
a variety of venues via the Loft, COMPAS, the Minnesota
State Arts Board, and other community organizations
throughout Minnesota for more than 15 years. Coffee
House Press published her book, *Because Why,* in 2006. She
contributes posts on feminism, mysticism, astrology, and
poetics to the multiauthor arts and culture blog
Montevidayo, and has won grants and fellowships from the
National Endowment for the Arts, the Bush Foundation,
the Jerome Foundation, the Minnesota State Arts Board,
the Academy of American Poets, and the Graduate
Research Partnership Program at the University of
Minnesota. Recent work appears in *Conduit; Action, Yes; We
Are So Happy to Know Something; Poetry City USA Vol 2;
Spout; ElevenEleven; Rain Taxi; LUNGFULL!;* and others. She
performs poetry rituals and other acts of intersubjective
communion in public and private spaces whenever she can.

SARAH FOX RECOMMENDS THESE COFFEE HOUSE PRESS BOOKS

Rough, and Savage
978-1-56689-314-5
Rough, and Savage is a lyrical collage of ancient fragments, fairytale, and both Korean and American history that is as daring as it is restlessly imaginative.

Earliest Worlds
978-1-56689-114-1
"Consistently wedding innovative technique with time-honored poetic tropes of light and dark, individual and cosmos, and self and other, this ambitious debut takes in a lot of influences but emerges singularly and beautifully."
—*Publishers Weekly*

Find the Girl
978-1-56689-244-5
"[A] dark but beautiful first book. . . . This is a vital poetry of the Deep South ripe with bones, blood and bogs, Snow Whites, Gretels and debutantes all stirred into a harrowing stew of lust, dusk and summer." —*New York Times*

Whorled
978-1-56689-278-0
In *Whorled*, Ed Bok Lee looks toward a global future, one where the dividing lines between state, religion, race, history, and culture have been blurred to the extent that the very idea of difference requires a new understanding.
A 2012 AMERICAN BOOK AWARD WINNER